CONTENT MARKETING REVOLUTION

SEIZE CONTROL OF YOUR MARKET
IN FIVE KEY STEPS

DANE BROOKES

First Edition: August 2015

Published by Giant Leap Media

ISBN-13: 978-0993369704

ISBN-10: 0993369707

For my mother, Pauline.

Thank you for your love, guidance and countless sacrifices.

"Dreams come true, but they don't come free."

CONTENTS

CONTENTS

CONTENTS

FOREWORD

By Matt Warnock

Digital Editor in Chief at Philips

These are difficult times to be a marketer. After decades of doing the same old things in the same old ways, the digital revolution came along and changed everything. Not only have functions changed, but the internet has also opened up borders. Your competitors are no longer just in your city, area or country; they're in India, Brazil and China.

The result is that 'the company' as we know it is no longer something of longevity. According to Professor Richard Foster from Yale University[117], the average lifespan of S&P 500 Index companies has plummeted from 67 years in the 1920s to just 15 years today.

The message is clear: you are replaceable. No matter what product or service your company offers, someone can offer it better, cheaper or faster. And they will replace you.

And yet, there are brands that make a mockery of that logic. People pay large amounts of money for a MacBook Pro when a standard laptop – a third of the price – would fit their need. A trip to the supermarket or drugstore reveals a plethora of soaps, shower gels and skin creams – most undistinguishable from the next – but Dove stands out as being pure, natural and gentle. IBM operates in a variety of hugely competitive sectors and yet none of its rivals come close to matching it for trustworthiness. I don't even drink Coca-Cola but I still associate the can of Coke with a sense of fun and good times.

So, in this ultra-competitive landscape, creating an emotional connection between your brand and your customer is how you can immunise yourself from the 'better, cheaper, faster' model. If people feel a true connection to your brand, if it reflects their values, and maybe even their sense of status, then not only will you stand out in a crowded market place, but customers may even pay a premium for your products or services.

That's where content comes in. Not brochures, flyers, banner ads or promotions, but valuable, remarkable content that creates an authentic experience for your consumers. Whether it's an educational how-to video, a game-changing whitepaper, a hilarious GIF, an expert webinar, or a broader campaign that spans multiple touchpoints, these are all opportunities to create an emotional bond with your consumer.

This might seem like a new phenomenon; the 'brand as publisher' is the hippest phrase being thrown around marketing departments the world over right now, with Kraft, Red Bull and Marriott the seemingly obligatory examples discussed and analysed at every single marketing event. But, as Dane Brookes entertainingly explains in chapter two, if you think content marketing is something new then you are very much mistaken.

Think you're immune to content marketing? Well, if you ever joined the *Kiss, Duran Duran* or even *The Beatles* fan club, then you were being content marketed to. Likewise, if you've ever picked up an in-flight magazine on a business trip or watched *The LEGO Movie* with your kids.

The beauty of all these examples is that they provide true value. It may be entertainment or education, it may even be monetary, but it places that value to the customer before the short-term needs of the business.

During my time at Philips, I've been part of that shifting focus; the transition from branded content – content that serves the business – to becoming a true content brand, which delivers a value to its audience through the content it creates and publishes.

As a key player in the new and emerging HealthTech space, Philips content often takes the form of whitepapers and technical blogs from thought leaders aimed at educating, informing and supporting healthcare professionals. At the same time, we still innovate in the consumer space with home health products; navigating that line between B2B and B2C can be challenging from a content perspective. Awards and recognition suggest that we're doing it pretty well, but this is because we made sure we had a clear and robust strategy in place before producing the content.

If big brands like Philips, with hundreds of digital properties and large resources find the demands of creating compelling content marketing challenging, then what chance do smaller businesses have?

I'm a bit of a health nut. I believe in eating as clean and healthily as possible, so I was overjoyed to find a nearby farm, on the outskirts of Amsterdam, which delivers organic, grass-fed meat. The website is easy to use, the service is quick and polite, and the meat is excellent, particularly their spare ribs. When signing up for the home delivery service, I provided details such as my email address and, once in a while – not so frequently I deem it spam nor so rare I forget who they are – I receive a newsletter from them. I look forward to it every time. It isn't a list of products or promotions; instead, it's a charming update on what ingredients are currently in season, information about different cuts of meats, and some tasty, seasonal recipe suggestions. The result is that I feel loyal to my meat supplier, and have often tried a new cut and even bought cheese or olive oil through the service.

In many cases, businesses are already producing (or have the potential to produce) excellent content. The key is developing a strategy for using that content and identifying the best channels for it to thrive and serve an audience.

Which is of course why you have bought this book. And what safe hands you're in.

I believe that marketers are terrible choices to lead content marketing programmes. They're too indoctrinated in the 'let's talk about us and push products' mentality. If you want to excel in storytelling, hire a storyteller. Dane Brookes is amongst the new breed of true content marketers – professionals who are pairing backgrounds in journalism, photography and film making with marketing expertise and experience to produce truly compelling customer-centric content.

By following Dane's advice in this book, you'll be able to devise a solid content strategy, with insights into how you can test, measure and improve. But then it's your turn to take the first steps into the brave (not all that) new world of content.

The famous US general George S Patten once said "A good plan today is better than a perfect plan tomorrow." He would have made a fine content marketer!

Matt Warnock, Digital Editor in Chief at Philips
Amsterdam, 2015

INTRODUCTION

"Content marketing is the only marketing left."

Seth Godin

We are in the midst of the greatest marketing revolution since the advent of the internet.

Within your marketplace, a leadership cabinet is being assembled and there is a space for you at the head of the table. But, you must arrive early before somebody else takes your seat.

This marketing revolution isn't fuelled by classic promotion or selling concepts; it is being driven by a cultural shift in consumer behaviour. Gone are the days when traditional marketing messages had critical power on buying decisions. Instead, customers want to make empowered decisions based on useful information, valuable engagements and brand affinity.

Welcome to the 'content age', where the most astute businesses are nurturing customers with highly-relevant content that goes way beyond the traditional sales funnel.

Right now, there's an opportunity to transform your relationship with customers and firmly position your brand as a market leader. Are you ready to rethink your marketing strategy and, in turn, attract more prospects, make more sales and excite brand loyalty?

Come with me and, together, we will stage our own content marketing revolution and dominate your marketplace.

FALL OF THE OLD REGIME

Traditional marketing just isn't working anymore. Consumers are no longer listening to advertisements and other promotional messages, which has led to dwindling returns on investment in conventional marketing activities. But why?

At a relentlessly increasing rate, consumers have been bombarded with marketing tactics of all types, from webpage banners and pop-ups, to video overlays and sponsored interruptions. Packed in front of, in-between and over the top of content they actually want to access, these disruptions have become so normal that most people no longer notice them, never mind take heed of the messages. Even when they're forced to wait or click something, the audience often just glazes over and waits, skips or moves on.

It doesn't matter how aggressively marketers push traditional strategies, without acknowledging the cultural shift towards information-based decision-making, they're in trouble.

WHY CONTENT MARKETING?

Content marketing taps into the consumers need to take back the decision-making process. It empowers consumers by providing content that is valuable to them on an informative, useful or entertaining level.

Content marketing involves creating, sourcing and targeting specific audiences with valuable and engaging content. The aim is to establish long-term relationships with new and existing customers that ultimately generate profitable actions. It can be used at every stage of the buyer's journey and crosses all channels, platforms and formats, including online, print, in-person, in-place, mobile and social.

While traditional marketing aims to sell with overt sales and persuasive messaging, content marketing aims to drive sales by providing content that will enable the customer to make their own informed decisions.

RISE OF THE NEW ORDER

The content marketing revolution is already underway. Look around and you'll see evidence of it everywhere in the form of free, high-quality content published by brands of all sizes, within all sectors. How about that free sales webinar you just attended? Or perhaps that complimentary recipe book you picked up from the supermarket checkout. Even that amazing free river event you visited last week to celebrate a cruise line's 175th anniversary. According to the Content Marketing Institute[19], nine out of ten brands are already marketing with content.

Content picks up the slack on the shortcomings of traditional marketing; it enables brands to influence customers and start building relationships much earlier, thus tapping into a larger pool of prospects, increasing brand awareness and qualifying leads at a much lower cost. In fact, research by DemandMetric[27] suggests that content marketing costs 62% less than traditional marketing and generates about three times as many leads.

STEP UP, YOU

The time has come for you to take your rightful place at the head of the table, but first I'm going to share everything I have learnt over the past decade working as a content producer, strategist and consultant for leading brands, across a range of industries.

Over the course of this book, I will take you through the crucial five steps that will form your content marketing revolution. From research and planning through to implementation and holding power, together we will cover everything you need to do to position your brand as a market leader through compelling, valuable content.

Here's to the revolution!

1

GROUNDBREAKING ROOTS

"History doesn't repeat itself, but it does rhyme."

Mark Twain

When I was at college, my history teacher, Brian Field, once said that history isn't just about the past; it's also the most reliable basis for predicting the future.

Brian was a mountain of a man, originally of Polish-German decent, with one of the most engaging personalities I have ever come across. I never found out if the accent he would occasionally slip into was deliberate or not, but along with vigorously shaking his mop of silver hair, it served as a great comic device whenever he was covering more mundane topics. In fact, the drier the topic, the more gusto and character he would add to his performance.

The reason I'm telling you this is because Brian's unique

teaching methods, such as his ability to capture attention, make content highly-relevant to the situation and engage with the audience, are also crucial components of successful content marketing.

Brian's bold statement about history foretelling the future also rings true when we consider the back-story of content marketing. Indeed, the explosion in content marketing we have seen in recent years is an echo, though considerably augmented, of highly successful marketing tactics used over the last hundred years. Despite the term 'content marketing' only emerging in the last decade or so, these tactics are some of the oldest and most successful tricks in the marketer's book.

Over the next chapter, we will take a look at some of the early examples of content marketing to see if we can learn anything from those groundbreaking marketers. How did *they* use content to help attract, influence and nurture customers?

THE FURROW MAGAZINE

One of the most cited examples of early content marketing is *The Furrow* magazine, first published in 1895 by agricultural equipment company, John Deere.

The free magazine, with a circulation of up to four million copies, was published to provide farmers with useful information and advice on how to become more profitable businesspeople, as well as learn about developments in agricultural techniques and equipment.

The John Deere company realised that helping to educate its target market would help their own business in three ways:

- To position the brand as an authority in its field.
- To provide a proprietary communications platform.
- To help customers make educated buying decisions.

By publishing the magazine every quarter, John Deere nurtured prospects and existing customers with a consistent, reliable stream of valuable contact between customer and brand.

The winning combination of an authoritative voice, a proprietary communication platform and valuable content, delivered consistently, has translated into more than 120 years of market influence.

The magazine remains in circulation today, reaching readers in 40 countries and 12 different languages.

*　　　　*　　　　*

MICHELIN GUIDE

In 1900, French tyre manufacturer, Michelin, developed the *Michelin Guide* in a bid to grow the automobile market.

Given there were only around 3,000 cars in France at the time, Michelin was operating in a small market niche. In order to create more customers, the company set out an ambitious plan to inspire more people to travel by motorcar and thus increase demand for tyres. Michelin distributed an incredible 35,000 copies of the first guide nationally, 11 and a half times more copies than there were cars in the country.

Rather than selling the benefits of motoring, the guide provided useful information, such as road maps, instructions for repairing and changing tyres, along with lists of garages, petrol stations, hotels, and restaurants. This useful content helped to educate and inspire the audience, as well as establish Michelin as an early authority in motor travel.

The Michelin Guide's restaurant star rating system is testament to how authoritative content can translate into market influence. The now world-famous Michelin rating system quickly became so influential that restaurants strived to be featured with multiple stars. In fact, the content became so valuable to its audience that the company started charging for the guides in 1920.

Still in print, the guide now consists of 27 guidebooks and is published in 23 countries.

*   *   *

JELL-O RECIPE BOOKS

When business was wobbly in the early 1900s, Jell-O owner, Frank Woodward, was considering selling the rights to the company name for just $35, at a loss of $415. But, within just two years, a clever content marketing strategy transformed the company's fortunes.

In a last ditch attempt to turn the company's fortunes around, Woodward embarked on a novel scheme that involved delivering free recipe books to housewives from door to door. The recipes included cost-effective, interesting and sometimes quirky Jell-O-based desserts.

By 1906, the company's content marketing campaign had boosted sales by $1M and subsequently led to a recipe series that is still published to this day.

The Jell-O success story was built on useful and inspiring content that aimed to capture the attention of new customers, encourage existing customers to think about the product in a different way and added a creative angle to an otherwise generic product.

Ultimately, the campaign worked because it appealed to relevant needs and interests of a specific customer segment, in the right way, at the right time.

* * *

BENCHMARK MAGAZINE

In 1913, engineering company, Burns & McDonnell, launched *BenchMark*, a trade magazine covering a range of trends, topics and disciplines.

For the past 100 years, the award-winning magazine has delivered content that has served to help customers make more informed buying decisions, while also demonstrating the brand's expertise in the field.

Consistency has played a major role in the magazine's longevity, with new editions published every quarter. Not only does this help to signify brand reliability, it also maintains a regular communications channel between customers and the brand.

The magazine taps into all stages of the buyer's journey, starting at the top of the sales funnel with early-stage educational content. This has helped to seed long-term relationships with prospective customers, nurturing generations of subscribers throughout their careers.

BenchMark magazine provides 100 years' worth of examples of how specific specialist knowledge can form the basis of valuable, sought-after content when targeted appropriately. Through consistent and targeted distribution of this niche content, Burns & McDonnell haven't been telling customers about their brand's value, they've been showing them.

*   *   *

G.I. JOE COMICS

In 1982, toy manufacturer, Hasbro, published the *G.I. Joe: A Real American Hero* range of comics in an effort to spark interest in the action figures, following a slump in popularity throughout the 1970s.

Hasbro hoped the comics would capture the attention of the target audience, generate interest in the characters and, ultimately, drive more sales of the toys. Realising the comics would only have any influence on their audience if the content was the highest quality, the toymaker teamed up with comic publishing giant, Marvel, talented writer, Larry Hama, and top artists like Herb Trimpe.

The clever partnership with Marvel also meant that Hasbro could piggyback the comic giant's market reputation and influence, maximising their content's value and exposure.

Hasbro went a step further in demonstrating commitment to their content marketing activity by investing millions of dollars in a TV advertising campaign to promote the comic. This is an early example of a brand amplifying the reach of their content by marketing their marketing material (we'll discuss 'amplification' in more detail later).

The comic book series proved to be a great success, eventually leading to an animated cartoon series, helping to make the action figure one of the best-selling toys of the past century.

*   *   *

BRICK KICKS

In the late 1980s, toy building brick company, LEGO, faced considerable market opposition from numerous big brand competitors and small scale copycats alike.

In a bid to retain its existing customer base and strengthen LEGO's identity, the company set about creating a branded community, using great content as the building blocks. The starting point of the strategy was the launch of free magazine, *Brick Kicks*, in 1987.

The power of *Brick Kicks* wasn't just in developing influence or building brand advocacy, the content also added value to the product in the form of model plans, building tips, games, activities and contests.

Not only did the magazine form a central point for the new community, it also established a regular and consistent communications channel with the target audience, further bolstering the brand's grip on the market.

Still in print today (now known as *LEGO Club Magazine*), *Brick Kicks* was the starting point of the LEGO content powerhouse we know today. This first venture into content marketing eventually led to massive expansion into other activities, such as in-person LEGO Club meetings, LEGO story microsites, numerous social networks and even a series of LEGO movies.

2

REVOLUTION IN ACTION

"Innovation distinguishes between a leader

and a follower."

Steve Jobs

"Are you crazy?" asked the suited senior executive who, for the purposes of anonymity, we'll call 'John.'

Sitting head-on in the large, shiny glass office he stared into my eyes and quietly uttered, "You're really suggesting we divert *this* amount of budget away from advertising and spend it on content creation?"

I paused for a moment, perhaps for dramatic effect, and firmly pressed back, "Yes."

John is a media company executive, based in Manhattan, and

he had called my company in to provide marketing consultancy for a new product launch. In this case, the product wasn't particularly new as far as the market was concerned and there were already a number of large companies with similar products. John wanted to set his company apart from the competition, attract more of the target audience and establish some authority in the product area. As a content marketer, naturally, I started thinking about content objectives and strategies. But, John, like so many other executives, wasn't initially sold on the idea of investing in content production, particularly if it meant the content wasn't persuasive or overtly sales-led.

John already knew a little about content marketing, but he wasn't sure just how much could be achieved, nor how other brands were using content strategy to help catapult their brands to the forefront of their markets.

"Ok, tell me what other companies are investing in content marketing and what are they getting out of it?" relented John, slightly.

In situations like this, I often draw on some of the best content marketing examples in the sector, highlighting relevant companies who are not only investing in content, but also reaping big rewards.

Who are the revolutionary thinkers in content marketing today? What brands are testing the boundaries of content power? For John's benefit, let's review some of today's content marketing trailblazers and look at how they are making it work within their own sectors.

RED BULL

Energy drinks brand, Red Bull, is widely recognised as one of the leading lights in content marketing of the 'tensies'. With 40 million Facebook likes and almost as many YouTube subscribers, they are masters of customer engagement. But what are they doing that is so special?

For Red Bull, their focus starts and ends with their target customers' interests, even if that means pushing their product to the side-lines. The company's marketing strategy is all about thrilling and entertaining its target demographic of 18-34 year olds, while placing little, if any, emphasis at all on the products they sell.

Red Bull realised there was a lack of media attention on topics their target audience was seeking out, including extreme sports, and saw this as an opportunity to connect with customers. The company set up Red Bull Media House in 2007 and filled it with more than 135 full-time publishers.

With a range of branded media that spans print, TV, online, mobile, music, games and cinema, Red Bull has catapulted itself into to a whole new league of content marketing superstardom. It's a great example of a brand being so good at its content that its output could legitimately standalone from their core products. Whether it's a live-stream of Eminem at a music festival on Red Bull TV or action, sports and culture articles in *The Red Bulletin* magazine, Red Bull's target audience is truly captivated.

Unlike a media company, Red Bull is able to use content to target the desires of its audience without being motivated by profit, sponsorship or advertising. The objective of the content is to offer an engagement return rather than a financial return, which means the audience gets a much cleaner, superior experience.

But why is Red Bull making such huge investments in content creation? It all becomes clear when you look at how much customer engagement their activity generates versus how much engagement a traditional marketing campaign could yield. For example, more than 40 million people on YouTube have tuned in to watch Felix Baumgartner's supersonic freefall from the edge of space as part of Red Bull's Stratos project. Even if that volume of people tuned in to a TV advert, how would they then engage with the content? Within 48 hours of the jump, Red Bull's Facebook page earned 1,823,690 likes on page posts, 62,976 comments and 211,810 shares.

Red Bull's innovative approach to content is perhaps not about return on investment, but rather gargantuan return on engagement.

*   *   *

FOUR SEASONS HOTELS AND RESORTS

Four Seasons Hotels and Resorts are so good at marketing that they have won a host of industry awards, but things weren't always going so well for the famous brand. The downturn in the luxury hotel market caused by the 2007 recession compelled the hotel's marketing team to rethink its outreach strategy.

Since 2008, the brand has been focussing on connecting with consumers and building brand loyalty to increase long-term business. In order to achieve this, the hotel's marketing team has shifted spend away from advertising and into digital content development.

So how did the Four Seasons marketing team actually go about ramping up customer engagement? For starters, they created a portfolio of special-interest microsites, such as *Have Family Will Travel* and *Taste* in order to supplement the brand's existing digital publication, *Four Seasons Magazine*. In order to further target specific audience demographics, they also created a series of Brazilian, Russian, and Spanish-language microsites. Pulling all of this together at one central point, the brand relaunched its website, with a major focus on connecting and highlighting its content output.

To maximise the reach of its content portfolio, the hotel produces as many as 3,400 pieces of original social media content per week, posting across 393 different channels. But, of course, simply posting large volumes of content doesn't automatically result in engagement; it's the brand's highly-responsive, personalised and thoughtful interactions with customers that inspires connections and nurtures those relationships. A famous example of this is when one guest tweeted that her hair dryer was too small and making it difficult to get ready to go out. The hotel picked up on the tweet and immediately sent a larger hairdryer to the customer's room.

The other innovative approach that the Four Seasons has made central to its content marketing is the use of a highly-personalised events programme for new audiences. For example, they sent Four Seasons chefs in a 'taste truck' across three states, covering 1000 miles, to entice new consumers with food and entertaining cook-offs. The same year, the team launched a Pinterest-based service called Pin.Pack.Go to enable consumers to better prepare for their trips by receiving travel recommendations from hotel specialists.

With such a personalised, ad hoc approach that serves 95 hotels in 40 countries, how does the business keep on track with its broader objectives? Despite an agile, high-volume output, all content generated falls within a robust global-led strategy, with devolved management across the portfolio. Felicia Yukich, Social Media Marketing Manager at Four Seasons Hotels and Resorts, Toronto, says: "Our unique approach has allowed a centre-led global strategy to be localised in meaningful and relevant ways at the hotel level around the world."

Four Seasons wins at content marketing because of its commitment to the customer experience. In marrying a high-volume, agile approach with compelling long tail content initiatives, Four Seasons manages to frame big stories within a friendly, small-world setting.

*   *   *

OPEN UNIVERSITY

Universities are hubs of exceptional-quality information, highly niche expertise and, in some cases, world-leading research, so it's surprising that the vast majority fall way behind other sectors with content marketing activities. Open University is one institute that has been bucking this trend in its creation and distribution of targeted content in a range of formats, on a variety of channels.

The University's iTunes channel has more than one million subscribers and has served more than 62 million free downloads of podcasts and teaching materials, all targeting current and potential students. In terms of video, the University's content commands a growing army of 45,000 subscribers, attracting more than 15 million views of informative videos that explain specialist concepts and demonstrate processes.

Much of the content targets specific audience groups at various stages of the buyer's journey (we'll cover the 'buyer's journey' in more detail later). For instance, targeting the 'Awareness and Discovery' stage of the journey, there is non-University specific content, such as technology tips and features on *World Book Day* and *International Women's Day*. Catering for the 'Consideration' stage of the journey, there are online and in-person events to promote learning and development, along with online questions and answers sessions and free taster courses. For the 'Purchase' stage, customer service content, such as guides, videos and podcasts demonstrate the product's value. Addressing the final stage of the buyer's journey, when the University aims to create brand advocates and up-sell, the alumni magazine *Open Minds* is distributed to 400,000 subscribers in print and eBook formats.

How does the University get content out to its target audience? The University uses social media to amplify content, across its highly-engaged network of 109,000 Twitter followers and more than 53,000 Facebook likes. The target audience is encouraged to ask questions publicly, which the social media team then responds to, often linking to relevant pieces of content.

Open University is the leading light in scholarly content

marketing. Its commitment to delivering value to its audience, tailored to the buyer's journey, with specialist information across a small, but targeted range of channels is a winning formula.

*   *   *

PHILIPS

In 2014, technology brand, Philips, revolutionised its marketing strategy in what it calls a "unique version of a content marketing programme". By adopting a 'real-time' approach to content development, the company is rapidly learning more about its audiences and responding with valuable content solutions on a huge scale.

In a bid to take control of the social conversations across five core themes (clean air; smart home; look good, feel good; ageing well and connected work spaces), the company has developed an innovative strategy that involves social listening and 'on-the-fly' content publishing. By developing authority within its themes, Philips has established an influential 'voice' within its core business areas (healthcare, consumer living and lighting).

But how exactly is it carving out its position as a thought leader? The technology giant reflects an unprecedented commitment to its audiences' conversations by publishing more than 5000 pieces of high-quality content per discussion.

The company manages its output in-house from specially created command centres, set up to power influencer-driven brand communications that pull together content, data and technology.

The content team typically produces three types of content in varying quotas for each conversation: 'Engrossing' or more in-depth content; 'engaging' content including co-created, user-generated and branded content; and everyday content such as tweets and blogs.

As much as 30% of all content is produced on-the-fly, with the remaining 70% planned long-form editorial material, such as research papers and documentaries; editorial blogs, press releases and articles.

A primary focus of the marketing strategy is to manage content in real-time, as well as amplify and distribute this primarily through influencers. Through a custom social media monitoring platform, based on Radian6 and Buddy Media, Philips is able to monitor key conversations as they happen. This allows the content team to quickly respond to emerging topics and discussions in their core areas with bespoke content. In order to help channel resources in the right areas, monitoring platform Traackr is used to help prioritise conversations according to who the big influencers are.

Philips' VP and Chief Marketing Officer, Damien Cummings, explains the shift away from traditional marketing towards a new content-driven approach: "Historically, we haven't done great marketing – we've put large amounts of money behind an image and TV campaign. But you can never build brand by doing advertising; you build brand by driving advocacy. And an excellent way to do that is via content marketing."

Philips' unique approach to content marketing centres around taking ownership of themes and dominating conversations about the things its customers care about. The combination of planned and real-time content, all amplified on a highly-targeted and measured approach, makes Philips one of the leading content marketing machines.

*　　　*　　　*

TOURISM AUSTRALIA

Perhaps leading the way with user-generated content is Tourism Australia. With a tiny in-house social media team, they have leveraged the help of millions of content creators free of charge.

The organisation's winning strategy hurtled it towards being the most popular destination page on Facebook, with more than four million likes, and the most visited travel pages on Google Plus and Instagram.

How can an organisation draw huge amounts of attention to its content without actually generating very much of it themselves? The model involves encouraging the audience to submit rich media content, such as photographs and video, which the marketing team then curates and pushes back out across Facebook, Twitter, Google Plus and Instagram. This yields huge audience engagement, with individual photographs regularly achieving tens of thousands of likes, shares, and comments. For example, one beautiful sunset photograph recently gained more than 100,000 likes.

By embracing technology platforms, such as mobile apps, Tourism Australia is able to further leverage the social element by creating truly connected content experiences. For example, one of the app's main features makes it possible for users to plot all of the locations that their friends have visited and recommended.

Interestingly, Tourism Australia has made a conscious shift in their target demographic. Rather than focussing on foreigners who haven't visited Australia, the organisation is concentrating its marketing efforts on people who live there and foreigners who have visited at some point in the past. This tactic cleverly leverages real-life, content-rich personal experiences and subsequently translates them into huge volumes of testimonial content, while simultaneously creating millions of brand ambassadors.

So what are the results? Tourism Australia's content marketing efforts have been attributed to helping generate the 6.8 million visitors to Australia in 2014 – an increase of 7.6% compared to the year before.

Tourism Australia demonstrates that content marketing success on a mammoth scale is achievable even with the smallest of marketing teams and little or no in-house content creation. With smart audience targeting and highly engaging, sharable content, Tourism Australia is getting the marketing message across in ways traditional advertising could never match.

FIVE STEPS TO SEIZING
CONTROL OF YOUR MARKET

-STEP ONE-

THE LAY OF THE LAND

3

RESEARCH

"To understand how consumers really think
and feel, it is vital to go beyond words."

Katja Bressette

Mike sat at the top of the dusty concrete steps, blindly gazing out across the morning London skyline. After everything he had achieved at college, in spite of the seven years' experience he had built up in the industry, regardless of the award he won last year, his boss had given him the worst job of the project. Mike had been asked to manage the research stage. Research?!

Mike had at least three years more experience than him, yet it was Alex who had been given the concept stage. The sexy, stylish concept stage. How many awards has Alex ever won anyway? How creative can a guy who wears the same grey and white striped tie every Monday possibly be? How many times has Alex stayed at his desk past 6pm without so much as a lunch break?

Mike stood up, dusted off his trousers and tossed his half-empty coffee cup towards the bin. Of course, he missed and had to go back and pick it up; it just wasn't his day!

"So, you got the research stage?" enthused Alex as he side-eyed Mike on his way into the building.

"Yes I did. What did you get?" Mike asked, playing dumb in an attempting to conceal his seething.

"I got the bloody concept stage." he returned.

As Alex was obviously making a good attempt at being humble, Mike thought he would return the gesture; "Cool," he said, trying not to look at Alex's grey and white striped tie.

"The whole project rests on you." Alex smiled, "Your research will inform every decision we make for the rest of the project. No pressure!"

Mike's heart sank as the weight of responsibility dawned on him. He had spent the last two hours stewing over the idea that research was boring, without considering how important it was to the project. As he walked away, he started to think about how much impact his task would have on the project's success, as well as how he needed to work on his team spirit.

In some ways, Mike's feelings were understandable. Research does sometimes feel like the least exciting and most arduous stage of a project. But, of course, Alex was right; it is often one of the most important stages of any project.

The good news for Mike is that research doesn't have to be boring; the bad news is it probably will be laborious. But, this is where we, as content marketers, can seize our first opportunity! The fact that research is time consuming and difficult means our competitors probably won't be doing enough of it. In fact only 11% of marketing decisions are made as a result of data analysis, according to Clickz[16]. Couple this with the fact that 81% of marketers (according to Social Media Examiner[95]) plan to significantly increase content production and we can see a real chance to get ahead by making more efficient, better informed decisions.

Unlike a lot of competitors, we will underpin our whole content marketing strategy with research. Not just research for the sake of it, but focussed research that will provide relevant, usable insights. This will help us to make smarter decisions from the outset, maximising the impact of our content and, ultimately, save us time and money.

Just in case you were wondering, the Mike and Alex story was told to me a long time ago by a client. He was 'Mike' in that story and, interestingly, is now Director of Research at a well-known cosmetics company. He clearly learnt to love research!

THE RIGHT STUFF

There's no point wasting valuable time and effort gathering intelligence we're never going to use, so we will focus our attention only in the areas that matter. But what are they?

Before we do anything, we need to get a clear picture of the current situation in our marketplace. We're going to need to find out what content is already out there, identify the hot topics of discussion, work out where people are looking for content, recognise which individuals and brands have the most influential voices, and pinpoint our main content competitors. Armed with this information, we'll be better placed to judge what kind of content the market will respond to.

In order to gather this information, we need to get a little closer to our target audience and the content community at large.

TAP INTO THE CONTENT COMMUNITY

Our content community is made up of everyone with an interest in our area of business, including prospective and existing customers; experts and authorities in the field; bloggers and commentators; and, of course, competitors.

A good understanding of our content community will give us an insight into the likes and dislikes of our audience. By watching, reading and listening to what people are saying, we will establish how they feel about important topics and what their values and priorities are.

SOCIAL RESEARCH

One of the best ways to get a reliable insight into our community is by simply searching social networking sites, such as Facebook[30], Twitter[109], Google Plus[40] and LinkedIn[56]. What are the main points being made? What are the key questions being asked? Who is answering the questions? Crucially, what content is being linked and recommended in response to problems and issues raised in public forums?

We can also supplement our manual keyword searches by monitoring relevant conversations in real-time by using social media listening tools like Hootsuite[44] and Social Mention[96].

BECOME PART OF THE COMMUNITY

Once we've identified what the community is talking about and the platforms they are using to communicate, it's time to start establishing ourselves as part of that community. Active involvement and participation in discussions will allow us to raise and lead the discussions that will help us to find out more about the opinions, questions and attitudes of our audience.

Remember, we will only get out what we put in, so let's make sure we answer questions as well as ask them.

AUDIT COMMUNITY CONTENT

Before we start thinking about our own content, it's important to get a solid picture of what is already out there. Here, we need to be looking specifically for content related to our product or service type, taking into account the predetermining reasons people are motivated to buy. Broadly there are three types of content to look for:

1. Content focussed on the problem or reason people might be interested in our product or service.
2. Content that helps people with the process of choosing the right solution.
3. Content related to the post-purchase stage.

CONTENT CONSUMPTION

Let's use the content that's already out there as a litmus test for our own ideas. What existing content (our own and third-party) is the most popular and which pieces seem to be sinking into the abyss?

Take a look at how widely the content is shared across social media using tools like Socialcrawlytics[97] and Shared Count[92], which track how widely specific URLs have been shared, liked and tweeted. We can also get a reasonably accurate picture of how much traffic third-party website content is getting using SEMrush[91], which uncovers a whole host of data about our competitors' digital marketing strategies.

We can use all of this information to forecast how our audience will respond to certain topics and content types before we invest any time or money into developing them.

CONTENT SEARCH

Luckily for us, not all of the content our customers are looking for is already out there. We can find out what information (or entertainment) they are looking for by investigating the popularity of relevant keywords used in search engines. The frequency that certain terms and phrases appear will help us to work out what content our customers are most hungry for.

Using Google Trends[41], we can drill-down on search patterns by country, region or city, while also revealing the most popular related words and phrases. By plotting a search term's popularity over time, we can identify which topics are 'hot' (growing in popularity) and which are 'cooling' (being searched for less).

Figure 1: Google Trends

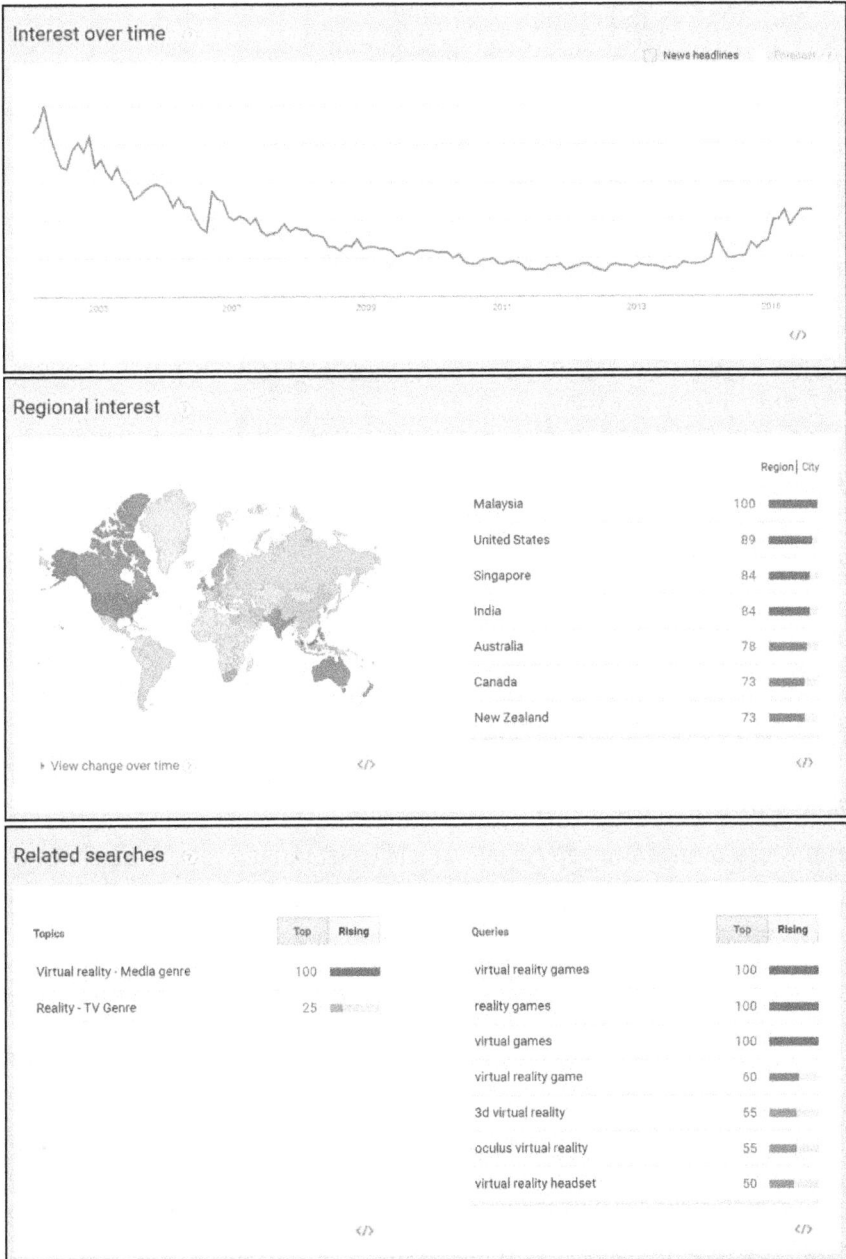

Interest over time

News headlines

2005 2007 2009 2011 2013 2015

Regional interest

Region	City
Malaysia	100
United States	89
Singapore	84
India	84
Australia	78
Canada	73
New Zealand	73

▸ View change over time

Related searches

Topics	Top	Rising
Virtual reality · Media genre	100	
Reality · TV Genre	25	

Queries	Top	Rising
virtual reality games	100	
reality games	100	
virtual games	100	
virtual reality game	60	
3d virtual reality	55	
oculus virtual reality	55	
virtual reality headset	50	

Source: Google Trends © www.google.com/trends

Figure 1 shows results returned for a search on 'virtual reality', within the Google Trends.

We can gather yet more insight by using the 'forecast' option in the viewing panel. This reveals predictions for future search volumes, which can help us to generate ideas around topics that are likely to become more popular over time, thus pre-empting our audience's content needs in advance of our competitors.

CHANNELS, PLATFORMS & FORMATS

What websites and social networks is our community using to access specific content types (e.g. videos, blogs, PDF guides, etc.)?

Again, by using social reach monitoring tools like Socialcrawlytics[97] and Shared Count[92], we can find out which content types and channels are most popular.

IDENTIFY INFLUENCERS

Engaging with the most dominant and persuasive voices in the market is one of the top three priorities of most content marketers, according to Curata[24]. We call these voices, which can be individuals, groups or brands, 'influencers'.

The two main benefits of engaging with influencers are: increasing our brand profile (by association); and giving our content the biggest potential for amplification (i.e. sharing and reaching large volumes of target customers) across the internet. Influencers, as the name suggests, have the power to evoke certain thoughts, values and actions among the target group, so it is important that we know who they are and, ideally, have them on our side.

As we research our community more, we will start to see which individuals and brands have the most valued, authoritative voices in the field. We can also use systems like Klout[53] to identify and rank influencers according to specific topics, which we can then compare against our own influence ranking.

CONTENT COMPETITORS

Our competitors in content marketing may not be the same as our competitors in business. Who is making the most noise and gaining the most engagements with customers on websites, blogs and social media? These are the voices we will be competing with when we start to publish content, so we need to gather as much information about them as possible.

Using Google Alerts[36], we can arrange to receive notifications when new relevant content is published anywhere on the internet. If necessary, we can even keep tabs on specific authors and domain names.

If we already have some of our own content out there, we can also compare how it's performing against other leading voices in our community, using tools like QuickSprout[79].

As we give more attention to what's happening in our community, we'll start to see the same content producers popping up over and over again. There may be one clear leader, or there may be a few. Gather as much information as possible about their content activities, including:

1. How frequently they are publishing.
2. Their specific focuses and niche topics.
3. The volume of content they have available.
4. How their content is received by the community.
5. Any obvious gaps in their provision.
6. How much of their content relates to current market issues and trends.

*   *   *

High-quality research is one of the most important weapons we will ever have in our content marketing armoury. Not only will it help us to better target our efforts and therefore save valuable resources, it will also highlight those big opportunities where we can make an impact.

The revolution we are planning in our marketplace will be bolstered by the intelligence we gather at the start and throughout the process. Don't be put off by what might seem like an arduous and complex task; focussing our research in the areas we have discussed will pay dividends later.

REVOLUTIONARY DIRECTIVES

1. Identify the hot topics of discussion in your community.
2. Gather intelligence about the leading content producers.
3. Investigate relevant keyword search trends.

4

INVENTORY & AUDIT

"Productivity is never an accident. It is always the result of a commitment to excellence, intelligent planning, and focussed effort."

Paul J. Meyer

Most of the companies I help with content strategy have already ventured into content marketing to some degree before I get involved.

A lot of these companies, particularly the bigger ones, have quite a lot of branded content out there, but don't have a handle on exactly how much or where it all lives.

As part of a quest to cover space, own conversations and take control of their markets, many pump out lots of different types of content in large volumes. The problem is, there are rarely appropriate tracking systems in place to monitor this content over the course of its life. This is irresponsible publishing because poor-quality, useless and out of date content can be just as damaging to the brand as good content can be rewarding.

We don't want to fall into this trap, so we need to do some grunt work at the outset by inventorying and auditing everything we currently have. We will then put in place appropriate mechanisms to safeguard our brand from content-gone-rogue.

CONTENT INVENTORY

First of all, we need to create an inventory of all existing content. This involves cataloguing every single piece (whatever the format, purpose or age), and recording the following information for each:

- Content ID (give it a unique number for reference purposes).
- Name (the title of the content, e.g. 'Top Tips on SEO').
- Content type (e.g. blog post, web page, leaflet).
- Location (URL or physical location).
- Format (e.g. video, text, eBook, etc.).
- Publish status (is this currently available? YES/NO).
- Content owner (who in the business is responsible for this content?).

There are a number of online tools that can help with our content inventory, such as Screaming Frog[89] and Blaze[7], but, personally, I prefer to create the inventory manually, using a Microsoft Excel spreadsheet or a Google Doc[38].

Figure 2: Example content audit and inventory worksheet

ID#	NAME	CONTENT TYPE	LOCATION	FORMAT	PUBLISHED	OWNER	REVIEW BY	ACTION
101	Top 10 tips on SEO	Blog post	www.example.com/...	Webpage/HTML	Y	A.E. SMITH	10.10.17	REVIEW
102	Content Marketing into	Video	www.example.com/...	FLV	Y	F. WILLIAMS	10.10.17	REVIEW
103	State of the Creation	Whitepaper	www.example.com/...	PDF	Y	I.M. SMITH	10.10.17	RETAIN
104	Intro to making money online	Podcast	www.example.com/...	MP3	N	J.M. CULL	05.03.16	REVIEW
105	Myth killers: Who wants	Blog post	www.example.com/...	Webpage/HTML	Y	E. McManus	05.03.17	RETAIN
106	Dave Cartwright interview	Podcast	www.example.com/...	MP3	Y	A.E. SMITH	10.10.17	REVIEW
107	Welcome to the content	SlideShare	www.example.com/...	PPT	Y	J. WANG	10.10.17	REVIEW
108	Grant Cardone interview	Podcast	www.example.com/...	MP3	Y	C.P. MORTIMER	10.10.17	RETAIN
109	How to figure out the	Video	www.example.com/...	MPEG 4	N	K. DOWN	05.03.16	REVIEW
110	Get up, stay up	Blog post	www.example.com/...	Webpage	Y	D. HOLT	05.03.17	RETAIN
111	The future of virtual	Whitepaper	www.example.com/...	PDF	Y	D. HOLT	10.10.17	REVIEW
112	Top 3 ways to improve	Flyer	www.example.com/...	Print leaflet	Y	K. DOWN	10.10.17	REVIEW
113	Content Marketing Rev	eBook	www.example.com/...	PDF	Y	I.M. SMITH	10.10.17	RETAIN
114	Life fixer: who wants	Email episode	www.example.com/...	Email	Y	J.M. CULL	05.03.16	REMOVE
115	How to make best use	Manual	www.example.com/...	PDF	Y	F. WILLIAMS	05.03.17	RETAIN
116	The only links you'll	Links page	www.example.com/...	Webpage/HTML	Y	J. TURPIN	10.10.17	REVIEW
117	Oculus Fox: The magazine	Magazine	www.example.com/...	Print mag	N	J. COOK	10.10.17	REVIEW
118	Oculus Fox: The magazine	Magazine	www.example.com/...	Print mag	N	A.E. SMITH	10.10.17	RETAIN
119	Oculus Fox: The magazine	Magazine	www.example.com/...	Print mag	Y	D. HOLT	05.03.16	REVIEW
120	Oculus Fox: The magazine	Magazine	www.example.com/...	Print mag	Y	K. DOWN	10.10.17	RETAIN
121	Train the trainer: a live	Webinar	www.example.com/...	Quicktime	Y	C.P. MORTIMER	10.10.17	REMOVE
122	The future of content	Infographic	www.example.com/...	PNG	N	E. McManus	10.10.17	REVIEW
123	The history of content	Infographic	www.example.com/...	PNG	N	J. WANG	10.10.17	RETAIN
124	How to sell more of the	Infographic	www.example.com/...	PNG	Y	K. DOWN	10.10.17	REVIEW
125	Facebook: is it the best	Case study	www.example.com/...	Webpage/HTML	Y	J.M. CULL	05.03.16	RETAIN
126	Free stock photography	Stock photos	www.example.com/...	JPG	Y	I.M. SMITH	05.03.17	REMOVE

CONTENT AUDIT

Once we have completed the inventory, the next stage is to audit our content. This involves assessing and grading every item according to its topical focus, quality, level of usage and how it relates to our overall strategy.

QUALITY GRADING

Look at each piece of content and give it a score (use any grading system you like, but I usually go with 1-5 stars). Here are the main questions we need to ask ourselves:

1. How well executed is the content (is it well written, appropriately professional to its context, etc.)?
2. Is the content in keeping with our brand and style guide?
3. How useful is the content in relation to its purpose?

USAGE AND ANALYTICS

Next, we want to look at how each piece of content has been used by our audience. Remember, success is not necessarily about large numbers of downloads, hits or hard-copy pick-ups. We need to bear in mind the size of audience it was targeted towards. If we created the content for a specific, small audience group, we should expect our analytics to reflect that.

BUYER PERSONAS

Map each piece of content to specific buyer personas (we'll cover 'buyer personas' in chapter 7), considering which logically appeal to specific situations and needs. Add the name of each persona the content applies to in the 'Persona' column.

If we find content that doesn't appeal to any of our personas, why does it exist? Equally, if any of our buyer personas are not served as much as others, does this mean we have a content gap? Do we need to better serve this customer group?

BUYER STAGE

Next, we're going to map each piece of content to a specific stage in the buyer's journey. Some pieces of content will map to more than one buyer stage, some might even fit into every stage of the buyer's journey. The point is, they need to fit *somewhere*.

Can we identify stages of the buyer's journey that are underrepresented? We're probably not expecting an even spread of content throughout each stage of the buyer's journey, but we may find that certain stages are less supported by our content than others.

STATUS AND ACTIONS

We will now look at each piece of content and decide what we're going to do with it, marking it accordingly in our database:

1. **Remove:** If the content is redundant, out of date, or irrelevant, we need to cut our losses and get rid of it.

2. **Repair:** Maybe the content is still relevant or valuable in some way, but needs some work to improve it or make it more relevant to our content marketing big aim. Remember to make a note of specifically what needs fixing.

3. **Replace:** Is the content valuable in principle, but flawed in its execution? In this case, mark it for replacement and add a note about why it needs to be redone.

4. **Retain:** This content is perfectly fine; we will leave this as it is.

REVIEW DATE

It's important that every piece of content has a review date attached to it. Depending on the type of content and the subject matter, allocate a sensible time for us to come back and re-audit it.

GAP ANALYSIS

Once we have completed the audit, we can start to look for content gaps. What else do our buyer personas need? Are we missing anything obvious? This information will help to guide content ideas later.

*   *   *

With a fully catalogued and reviewed content portfolio, we will be better placed to make judgements about new content and keep on top of existing assets. In the process, we're also likely to stumble across off-radar content that can be re-used. Just as importantly, we will also be more responsible publishers, with a clear idea of what content is out there representing our brand.

Most people are generally nervous about getting rid of content because of the amount of work that went into creating it. But, we need to be bold and remove the dead wood that is weighing down our portfolio. Think about the potential customers who may only ever have one touch point with our brand. Are you confident that *this* piece of content represents us in the best light? If not, pull the plug and start over.

REVOLUTIONARY DIRECTIVES

1. Document every piece of content in your portfolio.
2. Grade each piece according to quality and relevance.
3. Be ruthless with irrelevant, poor quality and out of date content.

5

BUSINESS CASE

"Success loves preparation."

Grant Cardone

When I first started my company, Group Dane, there was just me. Although I worked with a large pool of talented and trusted freelancers, they were not formally attached or dependent on the company. I had nobody to answer to, no directors, no managers and no permanent team. All decisions were my own and if the business floated or sunk, I was the only person that would be affected. This also meant that I could freely develop and pursue strategies without question or consideration. But I didn't.

Quite early in the process I decided that every big decision that could affect the stability or prosperity of the company should first be argued in a business case. Not all of the decisions I made were the right ones, but all of my risks were calculated and measured. The process of constructing the business case also helped me to clearly see the difference between risks and gambles. By my definition, risks can drive progress, but involve measured exposure to danger, while gambles are undesirable, as they rely on blind hope.

Over the last 10 years, working with companies of all sizes in the UK and USA, one of the main reasons businesses have given for not investing more in content marketing is a lack of buy-in from senior executives. Most of the time, this is because many C-levels don't fully understand what it is and how much it could benefit the business. In such cases, a solid business case for content marketing can be a game changer.

Whether we're creating a business case to help validate the benefits of content marketing in our own eyes or to win executive support within our organisation, our aims will be the same: to clearly present the business benefits, in relation to how they stand against the costs.

Below, we will run through some of the most important considerations relevant to our content marketing business case.

EXPRESS THE NEED FOR CHANGE

Firstly, we need to highlight *why* we need to make a change in the first place. Why should we not just continue with business as usual? If we can't clearly explain what is wrong with the current situation or where we are missing opportunities, it will be difficult to persuade anyone to agree to a change. For example, if our current advertising solution isn't delivering, specifically highlight where it is failing.

EDUCATE THE DECISION-MAKERS

Before we can present content marketing as a viable solution, we need to make sure the panel is qualified to make a judgement on our proposal. We can do this by helping to educate the decision-makers, starting with a lesson in exactly what we mean by the term 'content marketing'.

CLEAR DEFINITION

The Content Marketing Institute provides a useful nutshell definition that describes the process as well as the overarching motivations:

"Content marketing is the marketing and business process for creating and distributing relevant and valuable content to attract, acquire, and engage a clearly defined and understood target audience – with the objective of driving profitable customer action."

USE FACTS AND FIGURES

Let's demonstrate the scale of existing content marketing activity in our industry by using statistical evidence. There is a whole range of facts and figures available in various places online. As examples of the kind of stats that will help to support our case, here are a few recent figures:

- 77% of marketers have increased content production (source: LinkedIn Technology Marketing Community[57]).
- 71% of marketers are increasing investment in content marketing (source: Curata[24]).
- 68% of B2B buyers strongly agree that B2B vendors should curb the sales messages to improve the quality of their content (source: DemandGen[26]).
- Content marketing costs 62% less than traditional marketing and generates about three times as many leads (source: DemandMetric[27]).

CONTEXTUALISE THE BENEFITS

The best way to present content marketing as a viable option is to directly relate the benefits to specific business objectives, using relevant examples. As a starting point, we can consider the following goals, which are typically shared by most businesses:

- Increase brand awareness.
- Establish authority in the field.
- Build high-quality, qualified sales leads.
- Increase conversion rates.
- Enrich customer service.
- Retain customers.
- Harness upselling opportunities.

Next, we need to pinpoint specific areas of business objectives that content marketing could help to drive or support.

USE CASE STUDY EXAMPLES

Present the results of a content marketing-driven campaign, alongside the results of a traditional marketing campaign. If we've done a content-driven campaign already, we will use metrics from that, otherwise let's prepare some case studies relevant to our industry.

CONSIDER THE COMPETITION

Our business case needs to capture the attention of the decision-makers, so comparing us to our competitors can add some perspective. It also goes a long way in highlighting risks and opportunities that feel much closer to home.

Remember, we're forcing our point, so we need to look at more than just main business competitors, we should also look at the people using content most effectively in our industry; the best of the best. What did our research tell us about the companies in our industry that are covering the most ground with valuable content?

The key here is to demonstrate what our competitors are doing with content and pinpoint specific opportunities for our own company, along with the threats we face if we take no action at all.

OFFER AN OVERVIEW OF THE SOLUTION

Senior-level decision-makers usually oversee their companies in a very broad way, taking an overview of the key areas of business without getting into the minutiae, so it makes sense for our business case to do the same.

When it comes to details like content production and delivery, it is useful to have a clear plan in mind, but our business case need only skim the surface and broadly indicate how this will work.

Taking a high-level approach helps to keep our message clear without clouding it with too many distracting details. So, what is our vision or overall direction of change?

PROPOSE A PILOT PROGRAMME

Even if our senior executives see the potential value in content marketing, we might still struggle to get full-scale buy-in. Most likely, we'll be asking for resources, budget or reallocation of marketing spend, which implies long-term commitment and risk. Sometimes pitching a trial period is an attractive compromise for all parties; it gives us the opportunity to prove our strategy, but also means the decision-makers don't have to commit to long-term changes without home-grown evidence.

BE SPECIFIC

It is crucial that we're clear on what our pilot programme will achieve. We need to specifically outline what we hope to get out of the trial period. How will the business and its customers potentially be affected by this trial period? What exactly will it demonstrate? Crucially, what are the metrics that will prove our concept?

SET A TIME LIMIT

When proposing the start and end date for the pilot programme, we need to consider how long it will take for us to effectively plan, develop and distribute the content, while also building in enough time for our audience to discover it. The ideal trial period would be between 12 and 18 months, as this allows enough time to gather the evidence we'll need to identify trends and demonstrate impact.

SET ACHIEVABLE, BUT ATTRACTIVE GOALS

Think of the pilot programme as a test that we're able to set the questions for. Although we obviously need to make sure our challenge is achievable, we also need to make sure that the projected results are very attractive to the decision-makers. If we play it too safe with our goals, the impact of our pilot will diminish.

HINT TOWARDS LONG-TERM PLAN

Sometimes the perfect plan for a pilot programme can actually be too perfect. Don't be tempted to turn it into a full narrative with a start, middle and end. Our plan should lead the pilot to a crescendo-point that hits the target, but leaves a cliff-hanger that makes our decision-makers want to see more.

PREPARE FOR OBJECTIONS

Before laying down our case, we need to make sure we have considered as many of the questions and obstacles that could potentially be thrown at us. If we have solid responses ready, backed up with real-world examples, we will have more chance of pushing through our proposal, as well as saving face.

In my experience, the following are some of the most common objections:

"WE DON'T HAVE ANY CONTENT"

In my experience, businesses often push back on content

marketing because content production can be expensive. There is no getting away from the fact that good quality content costs time or money to create. But, there is no reason that this should put a stop to our content marketing plans.

The business almost certainly has a lot of great content already in existence, most of which is probably not being used. It is also worth noting that when we do develop fresh content, we can reuse it a number of times in a variety of ways. According to research by LookBookHQ[58], 60% of content marketers reuse the same content two to five times.

To help us deal with those thrifty executives, let's build some lower-cost content generation tactics into our plan, for example:

- Reuse existing content (repurpose and recycle informative, interesting and useful information).
- Make use of internal resources (colleagues and staff are a font of knowledge and experience just waiting to be tapped into).
- Collect, contextualise and republish other people's content (we'll look at 'content curation' in more detail later).

"THERE'S NOTHING INTERESTING HERE"

One of the most common limiting thoughts at this stage is that the company doesn't have anything interesting or useful enough to say with content. In almost every case, this is false.

The remarkable things around us tend to become less obvious the more familiar we are with them. I call it familiarity blindness. Take a step back and look at everything the business does with fresh eyes; get into the customer's shoes and view things from their perspective.

We need to arm ourselves with one or two ideas of how seemingly bland subject matter can be turned into exciting and engaging content. For inspiration, look at how healthcare, lifestyle and electronics firm, Philips, has created whole content campaigns focussing on light bulbs. Yes, *light bulbs*!

It's also useful to include examples of companies that have stepped back from their product area and are targeting their audience with exciting content that is not directly related to their offering. For example, think about the approach of Red Bull, which targets the demographic, without necessarily relating content to their product or industry. For Red Bull, it is more about brand building and association with exciting content. Could we do the same?

PREPARE ESTIMATED COSTS

Cost is always going to be one of the deciding factors, so expect to be asked for estimated costs, both for a trial period and for long-term implementation. Whenever we're forecasting costs, we need to qualify and support them with a return on investment projection, along with a comparison against traditional marketing alternatives.

It's usually a good idea to come up with a sliding scale of investment options, starting with the minimum cost for achieving a measurable and worthwhile return.

STRESS URGENCY AND TIMING

It's now or (probably) never. We need our business case to instil a sense of urgency if we want our decision-makers to act. If we're not able to motivate a response now, it is unlikely that we will be able to push this forward while there is still an opportunity to have any real impact in our field.

All of the points we make, all of our examples and all of the actions we propose need to be framed in the here and now. There is no reason to wait.

*   *   *

Whether we're working on a business case for our own benefit or hoping to win the support of decision-makers, it must be supported by strong arguments, relevant research and an attractive return on investment. Be totally clear on *why* we need to invest in content marketing, stating exactly *what* we want to achieve, *when* we need to start and *how* we intend to go about it.

It's *our* responsibility as marketers to adapt to the incumbent cultural shift in consumer behaviour. Only *we* can drive forward this momentous change in our company's approach to marketing and the business case is our first means of gathering the support we will need.

Of course, there will be barriers and obstacles along our journey, from budgetary black holes to decision bottlenecks. But don't be disheartened - some of the biggest revolutions in history were started with little money and no resources. But one thing every revolution needs is a strong and resilient leader. This is *you*.

What are you waiting for?

REVOLUTIONARY DIRECTIVES

1. Qualify all decision makers before making your case.
2. Relate primary outcomes to specific business objectives.
3. Propose a 12 month trial period as a proof of concept.

-STEP TWO-

PLANNING YOUR COUP

6

BIG AIMS, GOALS & OBJECTIVES

"If you don't know where you're going,

you might not get there."

Yogi Berra

Two years ago, I worked with a recruitment company based in London. I was invited to spend the afternoon with the marketing manager, Chris, to help identify why the existing content strategy wasn't performing as well as he had hoped.

"We've been putting content out for the past twelve months without much of a return," said Chris, before I had even pulled up a chair. "We've tried pumping content through most of the social media channels and we don't seem to be getting any response. I think the audience just doesn't want content."

I've had similar conversations with countless marketers in different industries and each time it has roughly followed the same pattern.

I asked Chris to print out every piece of content that he and his team had produced over the past twelve months and lay it on a table. For each piece, I asked him to add a Post-it note with the following details on it:

- The specific objective of the content.
- The kind of content it is (e.g. blog post, whitepaper, manual).
- The date it was published.
- The channel or platform it was published on (e.g. a blog site, website, SlideShare, etc.).
- The methods used to amplify or market the content (e.g. Twitter, Facebook, re-blogging on X site, etc.).
- The tracking and analytics mechanisms in place for each piece of content, along with figures.

The content Chris and his team had produced over the last year was mainly copy-based and it was all solid, well-written content. I could see how people might find the content valuable. But I wondered who, specifically.

Firstly, I asked what Chris meant exactly by "return". What did he want the content to do for the business? What did he intend each piece of content going out to bring back in? He was easily able to tell me that the overall aim of the company's content activity was to get the brand "out there more and become more visible to customers", but pinning objectives to each piece of content was more difficult.

Looking at all of the content laid out on the table, I could see that the same general goal had been written on every Post-it. Not a single piece had a specific objective, or indicated how it supported Chris' overall aim.

I wondered how Chris would know if certain pieces of content were 'working' if he didn't know what each piece was supposed to achieve. It's impossible to succeed or indeed fail when there is no objective in place.

In terms of content type, 90% was blog-related. This wasn't born out of audience desire, but was the result of a business decision to keep the content publishing process simple. How effective can any content strategy be if it is solely guided by what is easiest for the business? What is the point in creating content if it isn't presented in the way our audience wants it?

In addition, all of the content seemed to target the 'Purchase' stage of the buyer's journey; with nothing that obviously fit within any other stage. Without setting goals related to specific stages of the buyer's journey, how could Chris relate his efforts to "becoming more visible"? By focussing on specific objectives, it becomes much easier to align content with the most appropriate moments of the buyer's journey, while also presenting it in the most suitable format, across the right channel.

I noticed that Chris' publishing pattern was sporadic, with two or three pieces published at the same time and then droughts of up to three months before anything else was published. He explained that content was only produced when his team had the time to do it, so the gaps indicated the periods that team resources were the most stretched.

Publishing content to an inconsistent timetable isn't necessarily a bad thing, but schedules should never be dictated by internal commitments. Rather, our publishing timetable (or 'content calendar'), should *always* be focussed on key moments of audience need.

Most of the content was published on the primary channel of the company blog site, while everything else (two short videos and four infographics) was published on Facebook. The print publications (three brochures) were used as takeaways at events and the content was not accessible online in any form. Maybe the blogging platform *is* the right place for the content, but this tactic has to be grounded in research. How can the company become "more visible" if they aren't in the same places as their customers?

Similarly, the methods used to promote (amplify) the content was a two-channel approach: Twitter and Facebook were used to fire one-off alerts to let the followers know about the content. Without having specific targets in place, how could Chris ever be sure if his amplification strategy was actually working? Is it making the company "more visible"? Is it visible enough? How much is enough?

Tracking was limited to Google Analytics and Facebook Page Insights. For some blog posts, Chris would gauge how many views they had achieved, while he would look at Facebook Page Insights occasionally to see how much engagement they'd had with posts. But, how much could any statistic tell Chris about content performance if there's no target to compare it against?

It was apparent that Chris and his team were capable of producing high-quality content in-house. He also had a healthy marketing budget to play with. But regardless of this, he would never be satisfied with his returns without specific aims, goals or objectives in place.

The first thing I did for Chris was help him to establish what I call the 'big aim' (see definition below) along with a set of supporting goals and objectives. Over the next few months, Chris saw his first big content marketing returns in the form of massive audience engagement.

By having the right targets, Chris and his team were better equipped to concentrate their efforts in the right areas. In less than a year, he had revolutionised the brand's position in the market and catapulted it onto the radar of the target audience. Now, surely that's "more visible" by anyone's definition.

For the rest of the chapter, I'm going to guide you through the same process Chris and I followed. By the end, we will be able to confidently identify a big content marketing aim, along with the goals, objectives and tactics that will support it.

BIG AIMS

Before we go any further, we need to establish what I call the 'big aim'. This is an overarching mission statement that will outline the whole purpose of our content marketing activities.

When defining our big aim, we need to look at how content marketing can support specific parts of the wider business plan. It is crucial that we get it right because it will frame everything we are going to do beyond this point.

Agreement and buy-in from the decision-makers will make or break the project, so we need to involve as many key stakeholders and decision makers as possible in the development of the big aim. It is pointless coming up with aims if the people who will ultimately judge its success don't buy into it.

Our big aim should be broad, covering the bigger picture and written as concisely as possible. Aim for no more than a couple of sentences.

Example Big Aim:

"Our mission is to build up a reputation among UK businesses as the leading authority(1) in hotel web apps, while also being a friendly(2) and reputable company(3)."

GOALS

Next, we need to establish the individual goals that will help us to reach our aim. Here, we're looking for broad primary outcomes. The more carefully we define our goals, the clearer our direction will be.

Example Goals:

Goal 1a: Increase brand awareness.

Goal 1b: Increase awareness of our expertise.

Goal 2a: Improve customer service.

Gaol 2b: Improve positive engagement.

Goal 3: Improve brand perception.

OBJECTIVES

Our next move will be to take each goal and split it up into the steps that we will need to take in order to get there.

Each of our objectives should be SMART:

- **Specific:** Firstly, we need to clearly state what we are setting out to achieve. We need to be so clear that there is no wriggle room for misinterpretation.

- **Measurable:** We will only know if we have achieved our objective if we attach a value that can be measured, so always have a specific number in place (e.g. number of views, shares, likes, etc.).

- **Agreed:** All of the individuals involved in content delivery need to fully understand and agree to the objectives.

- **Realistic:** There is no point in setting objectives that we can't hope to achieve. Although we should be ambitious, let's take into account current market conditions and resources.

- **Timed:** Finally, we need to attach a time scale to the objective. If we don't have a start and end time, how will we know the right moments to judge performance?

Example Objectives for Goal 1a:

1. Publish one newsletter every week.
2. By 31st January achieve 2000 more blog subscribers.

3. Achieve 50 third-party Twitter tweets with both our #brandname and #hotels hashtagged in the next three months.

TACTICS

Once we have the objectives in place, we can develop the tactics we will use to pursue them. Our tactics will show the nitty-gritty of what needs to be done for each objective. Tactics are fluid actions and do not need to be measured.

Example Tactics for Objective 3:

1. Create a Twitter campaign around hotels and brand name hashtag.
2. Partner with 'hotel institute' Twitter account to syndicate campaign.

Figure 3: Big aim, goals and objectives (example structure)

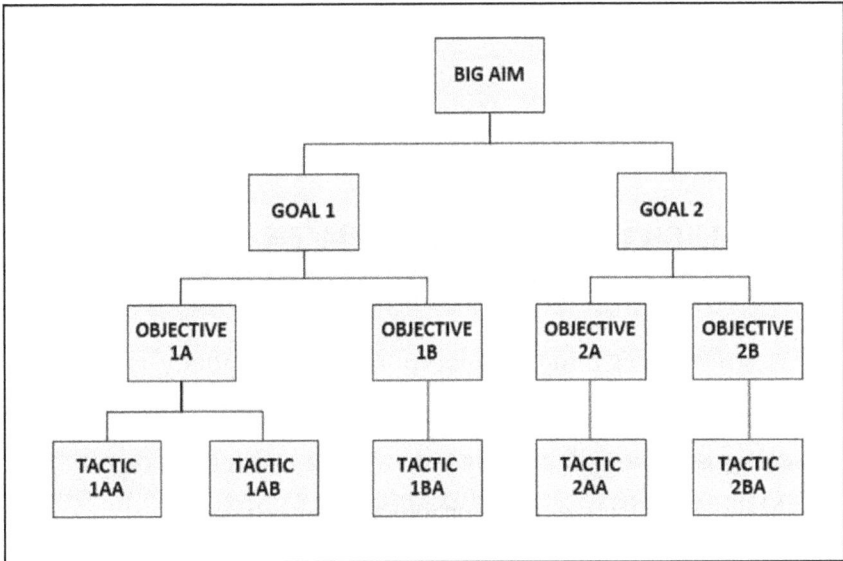

In order to get the biggest return on our investment, all of our activities must come directly from the goals and objectives that support our big aim. Not only will this help us to keep our strategy on course and make the most appropriate content judgements, it will also help us to measure the success of individual activities and the initiative as a whole.

If we're going to have any chance of making waves in our marketplace, we need to plan this out like our lives depend on it. If that sounds a little over dramatic, then you're not yet fully in the revolutionary mindset. Too many brands fail at content marketing because they are too casual about the motivations driving their content. Just fire an arrow half an inch off target and see how far away it lands from the board. We are aiming for precision, so put all of your energy into developing a precise strategy.

All in or not at all.

REVOLUTIONARY DIRECTIVES

1. Align your big aim to one or more of the company's high-level business objectives.
2. Set goals that will provide your strategy with clear direction.
3. Make all objectives measurable and time-limited.

7

BUYER PERSONAS

"You need to be everywhere your customer

or influencer is."

Fredrik Eklund

The agency guy was wearing a tweed jacket, a threadbare burgundy jumper, skinny jeans and black basketball shoes. The ensemble was finished off with a polka dot black silk scarf wrapped loosely around his neck and swept over his left shoulder. He was sipping a skinny latte in between nibbling the edges of a cinnamon Danish.

"Do you know who you're dealing with, Dane?" He said without breaking eye contact with his pastry.

"If you were marketing a 10 million dollar penthouse in New York City, you wouldn't target a road sweeper in Hackney, would you?"

Agency Guy sat back in his swivel chair and swung it to the right so he could see out of the large office window. He looked out towards Liverpool airport and pointed to a plane approaching the runway. "Do you think anyone on that plane is interested in your latest blog post?"

I didn't have a clue what he was talking about! I'm not sure if that was his intention, but he certainly had my full attention.

"You need to start thinking about buyer personas if you want to create truly targeted content." He said as he watched the plane safely touchdown.

Agency Guy went on to explain that buyer personas are fictional characters that represent main customer groups, which can be used to help inform sales and content strategies.

That was the moment, seven years ago, that I was first introduced to the concept of using buyer personas to create targeted content. Although initially sceptical, I was intrigued. How could imaginary people possibly help us with content strategy? Surely it was just another fad from yet another hipster digital agency.

At the time, I was working as a content manager for a property firm. It was a very traditional, conservatively-run business that certainly wasn't ready to consider using a methodology that involved using hypothetical users with fabricated names, stories and personalities. Unsurprisingly, the buyer personas project didn't take off there, but I was fascinated by the concept and spent the next year researching the logic, working on the development process and refining practical application techniques.

Over the six years that followed, I have developed many personas for companies of various sizes in different sectors, from universities to utility companies, from one man bands to blue-chip enterprises.

While personas don't tell us everything we could ever wish to know about our target audiences, in my experience they are the most useful way to understand and interpret customer behavioural patterns, motivations and goals.

Having a set of well-formed personas will help us to focus on exactly the types of people we are creating content for, why they want or need it, how they will access it and what actions it is likely to motivate.

How many buyer personas we need depends on how many distinct audience segments we need to represent. We're not looking for different *types of people* that make up our customers; we're looking for broad groups of *customer motivations*.

The key information we include in each buyer persona depends on the industry and product types, but they typically include things like:

- Gender and age range.
- Location.
- Educational and career level.
- Profession, specialism and industry.
- Wherewithal/budget/financial circumstances.
- Interests outside of the product remit.
- Shopping habits.

We can gather demographic data relatively easily from any customer or lead data we already have, by conducting online or offline customer surveys and looking at website visitor statistics (with tools such as Google Analytics[37]) and social media insight data (Facebook, Twitter and LinkedIn all provide built-in analytics).

Though demographic data is useful, we need to dig a lot deeper if our personas are going to be of any real value. It is difficult, if not impossible, to accurately attribute demographic information, such as gender and age, to the factors that motivate customers without directly asking our audience through surveys or interviews. After all, our aim is not to create an interesting representation of our audience; we are looking to create a tool that highlights key customer needs. Our aim is to elicit the ultimate motivations that influence buying decisions for our main customer groups, e.g. how, when and why the buyer decides to choose us or a competitor.

According to Adele Revella, author of The Buyer Persona Manifesto[11], the questions we ask when developing our personas need to be framed around five key areas of insight. Adele created the Five Rings of Buyer Insight to help draw out the key factors that will define our personas:

1. PRIORITY INITIATIVES

What causes certain customers to invest in a solution like ours, and how are they different from customers who remain attached to the status quo?

In other words, what is really on the buyer's radar? To use an IT example, knowing how old his system is, we may think our buyer is obsessed with replacing it. Meanwhile, what actually keeps him up at night is fear that the entire department will move to India. Too often, we arrogantly presume that since what we do is important to us it must be just as important to the buyer. The truth is out there, find it.

But don't confuse this with 'pain points' and assume we can simply reverse-engineer based on the capabilities of our solution. We want to understand the personal or organisational circumstances that cause our customers to allocate their time, budget or political capital to resolve the 'pain'. What happens to make this investment a priority for this type of buyer?

2. SUCCESS FACTORS

What operational or personal results does our buyer persona expect from purchasing our solution?

Success Factors resemble benefits, but this insight is far more specific and it's written from the buyer's perspective. For example, where we might be pushing our solution's power to cut costs, this insight might focus on where the buyer sees opportunity to reduce business risks.

Done right, this insight yields a far more specific and compelling set of factors than anything we can reverse-engineer from the capabilities of our solution. Instead of ending up with a ten-word tagline or summary that sounds just like our competitors, we will be armed with a concise statement of our customers' key expectations.

3. PERCEIVED BARRIERS

What concerns cause our buyer to believe that our solution or company is not their best option?

Adele calls this the "bad news insight" because it tells us exactly why this buyer will not buy from us. It could be internal resistance from another function or scars from prior experience. It could be a negative perception of our product or company, accurate or not.

We need to know where the barriers are and what's behind them. Who is blocking us further up the ladder? Where is that negative impression coming from, social media perhaps?

As a result, we may be surprised to find that our most valuable content focuses on overcoming these barriers and addressing objections that our competitors didn't know were there.

4. THE BUYER'S JOURNEY

This reveals the behind-the-scenes story at each phase of the evaluation.

Who is involved? How are solutions evaluated? How does the process unfold as the decision gets made? This insight tracks the stages that our customers go through as they evaluate options, eliminate contenders and settle on a final choice.

Behind-the-scenes, this can be a very messy process. Our key buyer persona may live in a complex ecosystem that includes all sorts of characters who have a hand in decision-making at various stages of the journey. Who helps our key persona and who gets in their way? We're often surprised to find that the people at the top of the totem pole have less clout than vendors assume.

With an accurate understanding of the journey, we can support our buyer with exactly what is needed at each stage. And we can confidently commit our resources where they will have maximum impact, be it social media, content marketing, sales engagement or something entirely creative.

5. DECISION CRITERIA

Which aspects of the competing offerings do our customers perceive as most critical and what do they expect from each one?

This final insight directly informs marketing messaging and content, clarifying the buyer's key questions and the answers they want to hear. But it's equally critical for sales enablement, as it identifies which customers care about specific features and why.

For example, if the buyer wants an 'easy-to-use' solution, we dig to find what they mean by that. Where do they want that ease? How do they go about evaluating which solution is easiest?

We usually focus on revealing the criteria behind three to five capabilities that matter most to the buyer in question. For example, specific product features, implementation issues or price versus value calculations.

Source: Adele Revella, The Buyer Persona Manifesto[11]. For more help with developing personas, take a look at Adele Revella's book Buyer Personas (2015, Wiley).

*   *   *

How do we go about eliciting the kind of information Adele identifies in her *Five Rings of Buyer Insight*? The only way is to get up close and personal with our audience. We need to conduct face-to-face interviews with a representative cross-section of current and prospective customers.

FACE-TO-FACE INTERVIEWS

Interviewing is the only reliable method of gathering in-depth audience insight. Being in the room with the customers allows for flexibility and enables us to adapt our approach based on the individual needs of the participant.

All of the information that forms our buyer personas must come from research; nothing should be plucked from thin air. Given that our interview intelligence will form the basis of our personas, it is essential that we ask the right people the *right questions*.

WHO TO INTERVIEW

- **Customers:** It makes sense to start with existing customers; they are already buying our products and services. It is important to focus both on happy customers and dissatisfied customers. Unhappy customers don't buy again, so it is useful to find out exactly how their behaviour differs from happier ones. Do they have different needs or attitudes? Are they just not our target audience?

- **Prospects:** Naturally, we will also want to know as much as possible about the needs, motivations and behaviours of our prospective customers. By definition, we don't have a business relationship with these people yet, so we will need to work harder on tapping into these groups. Any information we hold on prospects will help us to identify and reach out to potential interviewees. It's a good idea to start with any lead generation data we have, customer service queries that didn't end in a close and any social media interactions we've had with non-customers.

If we don't have any leads in to prospective customers, we can use free monitoring services like Mention[65] and Talkwalker Alerts[101] to monitor what people are saying about products and services in our field. It will take some further digging to identify whether or not they are genuine prospects, but if they are suitable, it's worth considering inviting them to take part in our research.

Remember that the purpose of our contact with these people is to conduct research and not to make a sale. Explain this from the outset and only talk about your products or services if they ask.

WHO NOT TO INTERVIEW

We could make life easier and save time by interviewing staff and friends. But we aren't looking for an easy life; we're looking for reliable representative data. Avoid interviewing anyone who falls into the following groups, because their answers will be at best skewed and at worst useless:

- Staff at the company.

- Friends and family.
- People outside of the target group.
- Non-customers with a vested interest (including supporters, haters and product reviewers).

HOW MANY PEOPLE?

There is debate about how many interviews will provide a reliable insight. Some, like Adele Revella, suggest that just six to ten interviews will provide enough data to identify trends, while Kim Goodwin, author of *Designing for the Digital Age*, suggests we need at least twelve. Personally, I have never interviewed less than eight or more than twelve for any one exercise.

ALWAYS IN-PERSON

All of our interviews must be held in-person. If we can't see the interviewee, we will miss out on valuable unspoken insights, such as facial expressions and body language. Plus, in my experience, interviewees are more open and receptive to questioning when we have eye contact.

THE PERFECT SETTING

A relaxed and comfortable participant is a more open and honest participant. The setting of our interviews is almost as important as our questions. The top three considerations are privacy, neutrality and seating proximity:

1. **Privacy:** When most people think about a relaxed and informal setting, they think about a coffee shop or a quiet bar, perhaps with a piano man in the corner. Although this

sounds mellow, it's not a good setting for an interview. We don't want any distractions, such as people walking past or noisy coffee machines, to interrupt our participant's line of thought. Always, always go for a private room.

2. **Neutrality:** We should never hold the interviews on our own premises. Psychologically, the participant feels like a guest and may be less comfortable passing negative comments.

3. **Seating proximity:** The seating arrangement is more important than most people think. The participant should always be seated nearest to the exit, with a clear route out of the room. It sounds odd, but, psychologically, this will help to relax the participant, as they don't feel trapped and can quickly escape the situation!

THE RIGHT INTERVIEWERS

Interviewing is a skill. If budget allows, get professional help with interviews. Not only will expert interviewers already have the skills required to tease out useful responses, participants are often more likely to be honest with a third party.

If hiring professional interviewers is not an option, we need to make sure that the people we choose are right for the job. They must have energy, empathy and examination skills in abundance (the three *E*s):

1. **Energetic:** Maintaining energy during the interview is crucial if you are going to provoke detailed responses. Energy

and enthusiasm are contagious, so a powered-up interviewer will keep the interviewee's mind active and engaged. Thinking can be strenuous; just think of the fatigue you feel after an exam.

2. **Empathetic:** Although the interviewer should try to avoid leading the interviewee's responses, building an empathetic rapport will help to put the interviewee at ease. Simple gestures like nodding, smiling and pausing make a big difference. Remember, when people are comfortable, they are usually more open.

3. **Examining:** All good interviewers are naturally curious and comfortable with going off-piste to further probe ambiguous or interesting responses.

FRAMING QUESTIONS

We need to frame our questions carefully in order to get the most expansive and honest answers. Our questions should give our interviewees the freedom to express their thoughts rather than simple "yes" or "no" responses.

Broadly, there are three stages of prompts to use throughout interviews:

1. **Example early-stage prompts:**
   - Can you please tell me how you came to...?
   - What were the events that led up to...?
   - What happened after you...?

2. **Example mid-stage prompts:**

- Was anyone else involved in your decision to...?
- Can you help me to understand how you go about...?
- What were the most important things you learnt about...?

3. **Example end-stage prompts:**

- Can you tell me how your views have changed since...?
- Is there anything you can add to help me better understand...?

THE DICTAPHONE IS MIGHTIER THAN THE PEN

Always record the interviews on a Dictaphone. You won't notice anything interesting about the participant's reactions if you are looking down at a pen and paper. After the interview, you can transcribe the audio recording verbatim and pick up on emotional indicators like tonality and hesitation. Do they really mean what they are saying?

Q&A TAG TEAM

Whenever I'm involved in interviews, I employ a system that my team call the 'Q&A Tag Team'. It allows all of the verbal and non-verbal responses to be captured without having to use a video camera (in my experience video cameras tend to throw interviewees' concentration and affect the quality of their responses).

For each interview, you'll need two interviewers working together and switching roles after each question.

This is how it works: Interviewer #1 should ask the first question, recording the response on a Dictaphone. While the participant is answering the question, Interviewer #2 should make notes about visible emotional reactions, such as facial expression and body language, anchoring these notes to certain points in the answer.

TRANSCRIPTION

Transcribing the Dictaphone recording isn't the most exciting task of the project, but it is worth putting in the time and effort to ensure you don't miss any key nuggets of insight. Along with the verbal responses, include information about intonation and use Interviewer #2's notes to include details about facial expressions and body language. This will help us to understand the underlying emotions connected to the answers.

*   *   *

CREATING THE PERSONAS

Once we have completed the interviews, we'll have a pile of data that will need to be sorted and interpreted. This may feel like an overwhelming task at first, but following a systematic approach will help us to run through the data and pull out all of the key information.

AFFINITY DIAGRAMS

The first step in piecing all of this together is to create affinity diagrams with the interview responses. This method will help us to organise large amounts of data into natural groups.

1. **Find key points:** Go through the notes for each interview one-by-one and write the main points on individual cards or Post-it notes. Take care to include the emotional states where necessary (including verbal, facial and body language signals). Each point should be at least a noun and verb, preferably a phrase. For example, one note might say "Product too expensive" or "Not sure if it's right for me".

    On each card or Post-it note, write initials or numbers that will help us to link the specific point to the interviewee it originates from.

2. **Group:** Put all of the Post-it notes onto a wall or table and group similar ideas together. It may be useful to limit the number of ideas that can be put into any one group so that the groups don't become so large that they become meaningless. Be careful to keep each group limited to one idea or motivation type, do split it down further into subgroups if necessary. For example, one group might be about 'Cost considerations', with subgroups 'Too expensive' and 'Value concerns.'

3. **Add group headings:** Write titles or headers for each of the groups that we have created. The headings should summarise the overall idea that the statement represents. For example, headings might be things like 'Financial', 'Logistics', or "Process practicality'.

Figure 4: Affinity diagram

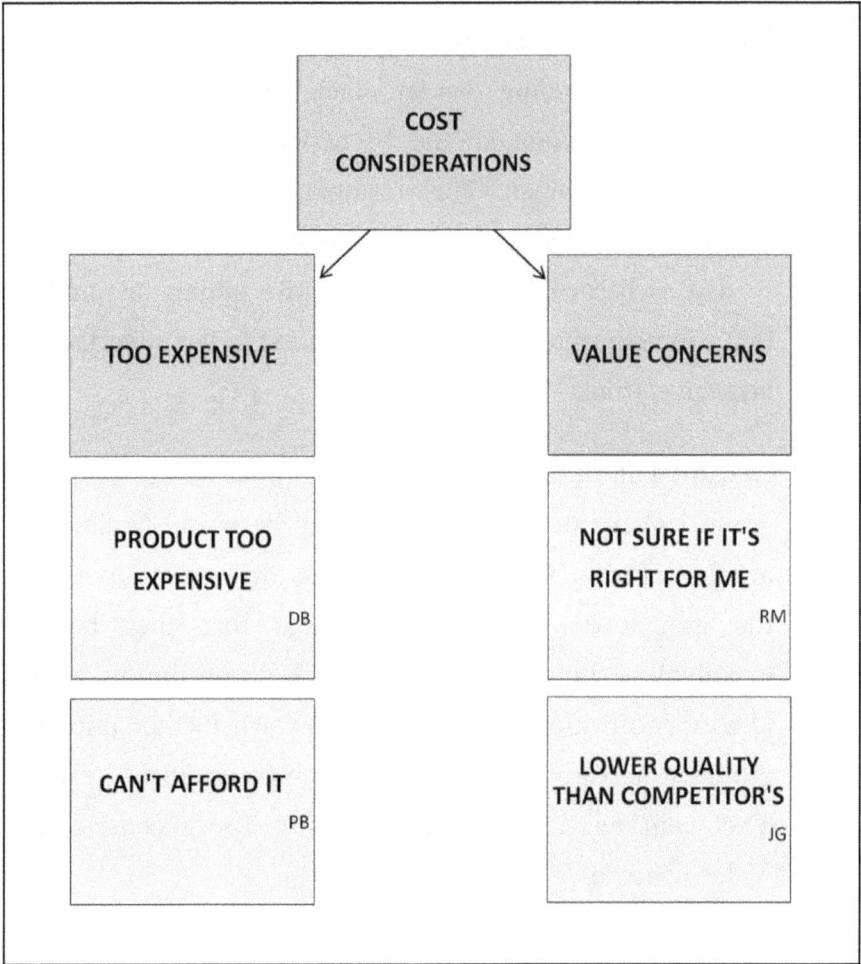

ATTITUDINAL VARIABLES

Once we have created each of the groups, it's time to start looking for patterns of attitudes and behaviour within each collection. We can do this by taking each group and placing the individual points on a variable scale, based on things like:

- Goals and motivations.
- Attitudes.
- Knowledge and expectations.
- Behaviours.
- Needs.
- Brand knowledge or awareness.
- Product awareness.

For example, if one of our groups includes points about price or finances, we might put these on a "Price sensitivity' variable scale.

Figure 5: Attitudinal variables

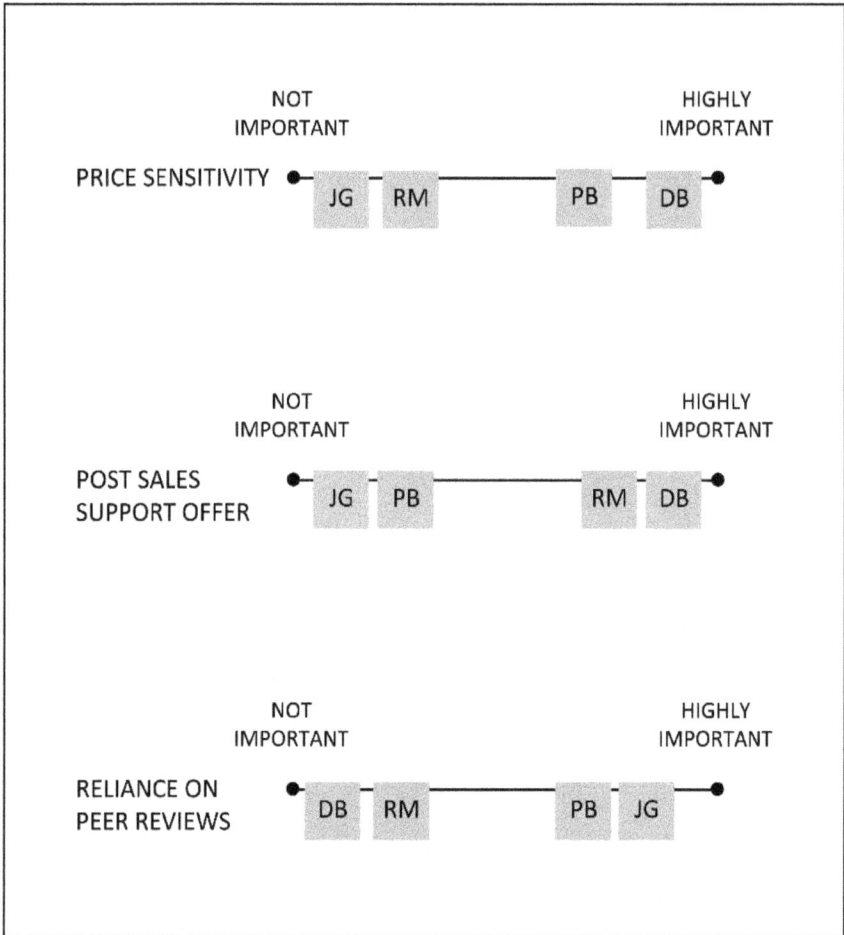

Once we have plotted where each participant sits on the scale, we will notice that the responses of certain interviewees consistently appear together on the scales. This is where the initials or numbers we added to each Post-it note comes in useful.

COMPOSING THE PERSONAS

Now that we have created clusters of ideas, we are able to use these groupings to work out which of our interviewees have similar behavioural characteristics.

For example, you might find that, across many of the scales, interviewees #1, #3 and #5 consistently appear together, while #2, #4 and #6 are also positioned closely. These groupings of interviewees will form the basis of our personas.

For each grouping, write a narrative around the common behavioural and attitudinal characteristics, forming a description of a person that embodies this group of interviewees.

Specifically describe motivations and needs and how they drive certain behaviours. Try to keep the narrative relevant in some way to content requirements; it is easy to go off on a tangent and write charming and fluffy descriptions that miss the key points.

Think back to Adele Revella's *Five Rings of Buyer Insight* to help prioritise the characteristics we feature in the personas. Remember that everything we include must be grounded in the data we have collected.

Next, we will bring each persona to life by giving them a name and photograph. This will help us to think about the personas as real people and more easily distinguish between them. Along with a name and photograph, include the following information:

1. **Demographics:** Based on the cluster of interviewees that formed the persona, create a demographic profile that most

closely represents the group. This should include information like gender, age range, income, location, etc.

2. **Description:** Write a few sentences describing what type of person they are, such as what they are interested in, what they like or dislike and anything else that usefully characterises this persona and sets it apart from the other personas.

3. **Motivation and drive:** In relation to our product area and content, write a list of the persona's key motivating factors. What makes them buy or not buy? What creates their need to buy? How do they go about finding a solution?

4. **Main enquiries:** Write a list of the personas key enquiries in relation to our product area. We need to take ourselves out of the equation; we're not looking for enquiries they may have in relation to our product; we're looking for more general interpretations.

In terms of presentation, aim for a simple layout that keeps everything on one page. You can download a free persona template on the *Content Marketing Revolution* website (www.contentmarketingrevolution.com).

Figure 6: Persona template

PERSONA NAME

Age: Profession:
Gender: Salary:
Location: Education:

BACKGROUND PROFILE:

Lorem ipsum dolor sit amet, adipiscing elit, sed diam nonummy nibh euismod tincidunt ut laoreet dolore magna erat volutpat. Ut wisi enim ad minim.

MOTIVATIONS & GOALS:

- Lorem ipsum dolor sit amet
- Adipiscing lit sed diam nonummy
- Nibh euismod incidunt ut laoreet
- Dolore magna erat lutpat
- Ut wisi enim ad minim

"A one sentence quote that summarises the persona will go here."

BEHAVIOUR:

- Duis autem vel eum molestie consequat, vel illum dolore eu feugiat nulla
- Eodem modo typi in hendrerit in vulputate velit
- Mirum est notare quam litter
- Qui blandit praesent fiant soll omnes in futurum
- Ut wisi enim ad minim lorem ipsum dolor sit amet adipiscin lit sed diam nonummy
- Nibh euismod incidunt ut dolo magna erat lutpat, ut wisi eni ad minim

WHAT I WANT TO KNOW:

- Mirum est notare quam litter
- Qui blandit praesent fiant soll omnes in futurum
- Duis autem vel eum molestie consequat, vel illum dolore eu feugiat nulla
- Eodem modo typi in hendrerit in vulputate velit
- Nibh euismod incidunt ut dolo magna erat lutpat, ut wisi eni ad minim
- Ut wisi enim ad minim lorem ipsum dolor sit amet adipiscin lit sed diam nonummy

At this point, we're already way ahead of half of all companies using content marketing! According to LinkedIn Technology Marketing Community[57], only 52% use personas to inform their content decisions.

We can maintain this advantage by using our personas to direct all of our content marketing efforts from now on. We will religiously ask our personas what they think about content ideas and publishing tactics and allow ourselves to be inspired by their needs and motivations.

For the first time ever, your customers will always be right there with you in the room to guide your decisions.

REVOLUTIONARY DIRECTIVES

1. Develop one persona for each distinct customer type (aim for between 2 and 7).
2. Identify common *behavioural* characteristics among your target audience.
3. Highlight what goals specifically motivate these behaviours.

8

BUYER'S JOURNEY

"We cannot solve our problems with the same level
of thinking that created them."

Albert Einstein

My old boss used to pull on a tatty old pair of brown brogues every time we talked about 'the buyer's journey'. I'm not sure why they were never re-claimed by their owner, but apparently they had been left in the office by a client a few years before. Perhaps a fluke, or maybe a gift from above, they fitted him perfectly. This was Graham's very literal and slightly eccentric way of getting into the customer's shoes.

Whenever questioned about it, Graham would say he wanted to feel every callus, every rub and every stone along the customer's journey. And it seemed to work; when he had those shoes on, his personality seemed to change, almost as if he was possessed by the spirit of the customer.

Graham wasn't just helping himself to feel more connected to the customer, he was also inspiring the rest of the team to think and behave as if a real customer was in the room. It's amazing how positive and inspiring conversations become when we imagine a customer is right there with us.

I'm not suggesting we commandeer a pair of customers' shoes, but we at least need to take big steps towards understanding the customer's perspective at every stage of the journey.

To a greater or lesser degree, every customer goes through the same basic journey before buying a product, it is just that certain stages take longer for some customers than others. Thoroughly understanding how different types of customers (as reflected in our buyer personas) progress through this journey will help us to recognise opportunities to influence (and even speed up) progression at each stage.

By providing valuable content, we can have meaningful contact with potential customers at all of these stages, but it has to be the right kind of content. Our task is to recognise what they need and when they need it.

In this chapter, we'll take a look at the buyer's journey, along with some examples of the types of content that can work well at various stages.

Figure 7: Buyer's Journey

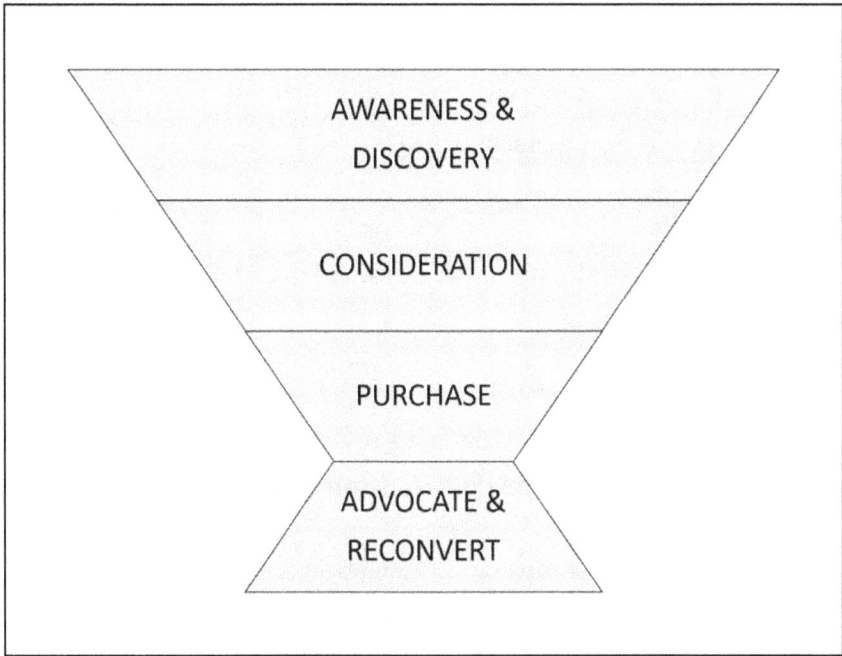

1. AWARENESS & DISCOVERY

AWARENESS

This is the stage of the buyer's journey where some kind of need or desire emerges. The customer probably doesn't know that a solution exists at this point and, more than likely, they will not have heard of our company.

Our aim at this stage is to create awareness of our existence, while demonstrating relevant authority and expertise. Typically, at this point, the customer is looking for lighter content that helps to introduce a new idea or concept. Here, we are aiming to inspire the potential buyer's interest in the topic.

Examples of good 'Awareness and Discovery' stage content include entry-level material that talks around the customer's emerging need or desire, such as:

- Blog posts.
- How-to guides (including articles, videos, etc.).
- Reports and eBooks.
- Diagnostic tools.
- Infographics.
- Whitepapers (mainly for B2B customers).

Our content should include a suggestion about the next step for the buyer. Calls to action at the 'Awareness and Discovery' stage should direct the buyer towards supplementary content within the same stage, or gently direct them towards content within the 'Consideration' stage. Either way, it should encourage them to engage with the content on some level, for example:

- Visit or download related content.
- Leave a comment or ask a question.
- Share the content on social media.
- Subscribe to a newsletter.
- Follow for more information on the topic.

Remember, our aim is to provide *useful* content; there should be no bias towards our products or brand. We are serving to educate the user, not necessarily provide the full solution just yet.

DISCOVERY

This is the most difficult stage of the journey for getting our content discovered by the target audience. The fact the customer is not necessarily informed about their need or desire means they are probably not yet searching for a solution at all.

It is important to search engine optimise our online content with keywords, title tags and URLs that take into account the fact that our audience is unlikely to be familiar with the 'correct' terminology. It's important to use plain English rather than the jargon that more qualified customers might be searching.

We need to do the same for offline content, such as print materials; it is important that we distribute our content in the places that our audience might be looking for solutions, rather than just the places that qualified leads go. It's about being creative with our positioning, as well as using headlines, taglines and text that entices prospects with limited knowledge of the topic. Get into our personas shoes and target the most likely places they will look.

We can find out what terms and phrases our customers are searching with free keyword analysis tool, Wordtracker[116]. *Figure 8* shows popular terms associated with 'content marketing.

Figure 8: Wordtracker

Keyword	Volume
content marketing	537
content marketing strategy	70
kudani content marketing	42
marketing content	33
salad bar content marketing	27
what is content marketing	25
content marketing magazine	24
min read content marketing	23
content marketing principles	22
content marketing titles	19

Source: Wordtracker © www.wordtracker.com

ATTENTION!

Regardless of type or format, all content should have headlines or titles that clearly communicate its value to the audience at their current stage. The buyer doesn't know exactly what they need yet, so capture their attention by telling them why they should look at our content. Why is it appealing? Who is it useful to? What level is it pitched at?

2. CONSIDERATION

At the 'Consideration' stage, the buyer is aware of a number of potential solutions. They are doing more research than before and feel they are informed enough to start to eliminate some of their earlier considerations.

Our goal at this stage is to help the buyer to find the best solution to their problem, as well as prepare them to evaluate our brand's offering. Ultimately, we are aiming to now start converting our audience into prospects.

Though we will continue to provide enlightening content, we will pitch it at a slightly higher level, with more focus on solution comparisons. At this stage, we're looking to demonstrate the best options and build faith in our brand, *without selling*. Types of valuable content at this stage include:

- Platforms for discussion, such as forums.
- Relevant case studies.
- Customer testimonials.
- Demonstrative videos.
- Tutorials.
- Comparison articles.
- Newsletters and eBooks.
- FAQs.

Our calls to action are going to be similar to these at the 'Discovery' stage, but now we want to encourage customers to engage with us, while continuing to push other supporting content and shuffle the prospect along to the 'Purchase' stage. But, remember, we're still not pushing our audience to buy anything yet.

3. PURCHASE

At the 'Purchase' stage, our audience is ready to select a product or provider and make a purchase.

They will now begin to think about the final points that will clinch the decision, such as pricing, practicality and availability of customer support. Therefore, our content should aim to reassure the buyer about our solution.

This is the stage that customers will be most receptive to more traditional marketing tactics, so our content should aim to balance any sales-focussed content and maintain the unbiased voice we have carefully developed up until this point. Content that supports the 'Purchase' stage includes:

- Case studies with a post-sale focus (what are other customers' experiences?).
- Customer-generated testimonials.
- Live in-person events.
- Return on investment forecasts and calculation tools.
- Pricing, package and offer guides.
- Guides about managing any associated post-sale costs.
- User support documentation.
- Functional tools that support the product.
- Discussions online about the product.
- In-depth tutorials.

The calls to action at this stage will be supportive of the sales *process*, rather than the sales *decision*. We will direct people towards special offers, discounts and direct contact with the company.

4. ADVOCATE AND RECONVERT

One of the main aims of brand building is to turn customers into loyal advocates. How can we make sure our customers want to be associated with our products?

At this stage, we want to encourage customers to reach out to other prospects and promote our solution for the greater good. Post-sale, the valuable content that will enrich the experience of customers will prepare them for advocacy and upselling.

USER-GENERATED CONTENT

Nothing persuades customers more than the recommendations of existing customers. Equally nothing inspires loyalty more than a feeling of community. By encouraging customers to create and share their own content relevant to your product not only empowers existing customers to use their voice to endorse our product, it inspires community among our customers and, crucially, it has authenticity written all over it.

CONSISTENT MESSAGES

The content that we have provided throughout the cycle so far should have helped to establish a consistent, authoritative and trusted voice. A lot of companies fall down by failing to nurture post-sale relationships. We must continue to provide valuable and relevant content that will help us to up-sell and transform our customers into brand advocates.

Given customers trust the opinions of other customers more than anything the business tells them, we want to encourage them to shout about their positive experiences. At this stage, one of our focuses should be highly-shareable content that rewards our customers for sharing by transferring street cred or authority. Examples of this kind of content include:

- Aspirational or 'showy' content (look at me!).
- Contests and giveaways.
- Games.
- Special offers.
- Hints, tricks and life hacks related to the brand.

SUBSCRIBE OR DIE

It is essential to capitalise on the relationship we have worked so hard to nurture by keeping a communications channel open. If they haven't signed up already, it's important to encourage our customers to subscribe to receive notifications about our post-sale content.

*　　　　*　　　　*

Get infatuated with the buyer's journey! Live it and breathe it. Immerse yourself in the customer's world and get to know their struggles and triumphs inside out. What are the key pivotal moments in the journey? Where do they fall down and how do they get back up?

Do whatever it takes to stay focussed on that journey. Personally, I find having a giant poster of the buyer's journey on the wall in my office helps. It forces me to focus my mind and keep everything that's unrelated to the journey off my desk. Remember, if it isn't important to the journey, it isn't content; it's clutter!

Try it yourself. Hang it on your wall. Put it in your office, in the bathroom, above your bed, even put it on a business card and keep it in your wallet! Never lose sight of the journey. It's our obligation as a content marketer to walk this journey with our customers.

Sounds obsessive? Sure. But tell me the story of a revolutionary that wasn't obsessed with their mission and I'll show you a fictional tale.

REVOLUTIONARY DIRECTIVES

1. Identify our buyer personas' main needs at each stage of the journey.
2. Ensure all content is assigned to a specific stage, with a focus on moving customers through the cycle.
3. Determine which content types will be the most appealing at each stage.

9

CONTENT CALENDAR

"Success is simple: do what's right, the right way,

at the right time."

Arnold H. Glasow

A few years ago, I managed an editorial department at one of the biggest open-access science publishing companies in the world. Every day, we published dozens of high-profile, peer-reviewed academic papers and articles. The majority of the content represented the latest, cutting-edge scientific research, so we were under considerable pressure to deliver to tight deadlines. Nevertheless, the schedule was carefully managed and nothing ever entered the workflow that we couldn't commit to. When it came to new journal launches, they were carefully planned, marketed and published at the optimal time for both the topic and the academic audience. It was a slick, efficient operation that delivered high-quality content every time.

As content marketers, we aren't a publishing company and we won't be outputting anywhere near the volume of a top publishing house, but we can certainly learn a lot from their operations. How can we mirror their efficiency, consistency and timing?

We have already spent a lot of time investigating our audience's needs at various stages of their journey. Now we need to think about how we can practically deliver it at these critical moments, with the most efficient and consistent approach. We'll achieve this with the help of a carefully prepared publishing schedule, which we'll call our 'content calendar'.

SELECTING THE RIGHT SYSTEM

Whether it's a paper-based diary or dedicated computer software, we need to have a system in place to manage our content calendar. It doesn't matter what tools we choose, as long as they are appropriate for the scale of our activities.

For content marketing plans where the production process is simple and output volumes are moderate, a basic spreadsheet or Outlook calendar is probably suitable. It's also worth thinking about basic online diaries and organisers, particularly for plans that involve slightly more content production. Personally, I've managed reasonably-sized content schedules quite comfortably using Google Calendar, with automated alerts set up for each piece at key intervals.

For those content marketing strategies that involve high

volumes of mixed-media, multi-supplier production, we'll need a more robust management system. There are a variety of options available, but my personal favourite is an online system called Gather Content[33]. This system can be used to help plan, diarise and store content prior to publication, while also making it easier to manage collaborations between multiple content producers and reviewers.

NOMINATE OWNERSHIP

Quite possibly, our content will be generated by a number of different people within our organisation and maybe even by outsourced content providers. While this approach often bears fruit in the shape of high-quality, rich, varied content, it also means the workflow feed can become fragmented. So where does the buck stop if content isn't flowing consistently? Who will take responsibility? Why not give one person within the company (maybe you) ownership of the content calendar and workflow? If no single person has responsibility, there will be no one to keep us on course.

ALLOCATE PRODUCERS & SOURCES EARLY

For each piece of content in our plan, we will allocate the individual or agency that will produce it. But we must always ensure that production deadlines are agreed with all parties before the item goes into the content calendar. Although we're going to need to switch things around occasionally, we want these switches to be driven by customer need and market opportunities rather than administrative or resourcing issues.

I also find it useful to build advance notices about production deadlines into the calendar, which allows time for producers to be reminded of agreed timescales. It's better to send a reminder early than chase late!

TO COMMIT OR NOT TO COMMIT?

The amount of content we plan to distribute throughout the year should be ambitious, but also achievable. Every item we put into the content calendar is a commitment to publishing on that date, at that time, and we need to respect it.

The best way to ensure we stick to the calendar is to only commit content items if we are confident we have the resources and/or budget required for them to be delivered.

SET DEADLINES

For every piece of content we schedule, we'll attach three key dates. One to make sure it is actually created, one to make sure it gets published at the right time and one to monitor it post-publishing:

1. **Production deadline:** Take into account how much time and resources production of the content will require and set an achievable deadline. Remember to be realistic: stretching is good, but breaking is bad.

2. **Publication date:** Make sure we allow enough time after the production date for it to be checked, reviewed and

amended. A lot of people make the mistake of not allowing enough time for this. As a general rule of thumb, I tend to allow at least a third of the time that was allocated to production.

3. **Review date:** Adding a review date helps to ensure the content isn't just published and forgotten about. Out of date content can be just as damaging to our brand as good content can be rewarding. The review date will depend on the type of content, its content and the subject matter. Are there any events or dates that put the content at risk of being inaccurate or dated?

PLAN FOR THEMES & SERIES

Producing content as part of a theme or series is a great way of getting our teeth into an important topic, while maintaining audience contact over a longer period. Think video or blog series, for example. The great thing about content-in-series is that we're able to build a relationship with the audience over a longer period, while also demonstrating our brand's consistent and reliable principles (if these are our values when it comes to content, it must be the same when it comes to our products, right?). But we can obviously only make this impression if our publishing pattern is actually consistent. For example, maybe we'll publish instalments on the same day, every week.

CONSIDER THE CALENDAR YEAR

It's important that we plan and organise our content publishing around key events, dates, product launches and any sector or regulatory patterns that might apply. How is the buyer's journey affected by these dates?

For example, in the case of a university, the undergraduate applicant's journey is broadly mapped to the academic year and events that are specific to the sector, such as open day seasons, application windows, clearing, etc. As a result, prospects require specific content at certain times of the year.

WHAT ABOUT BUSINESS COMMITMENTS?

Think about our business calendar. How will our resources be affected during busy periods? If we're producing content in-house, it's important we account for the times resources are likely to be stretched thin. For instance, if the annual report or a new product launch is likely to cause bottlenecks, it is best to avoid content blackouts and backlogs by preparing content well in advance.

*   *   *

Given that 70% of content marketers lack consistency in their strategy (Altimeter research[3]), there is a real opportunity to get ahead of your competitors with a well-planned content calendar.

Strong discipline and an acute understanding of the market will be your new best friends. Aim for a well-informed plan that is fluid enough to respond to new opportunities as they arise. But remember, there is a fine balance to strike between commitment to the schedule and pragmatism in your approach.

Respect your content calendar, after all, it is the roadmap towards a more consistent, efficient and resourceful operation.

REVOLUTIONARY DIRECTIVES

1. Use a calendar management system that is appropriate to the volume of activity.
2. Assign one person to take ownership of the content calendar and production workflow.
3. Be ambitious, but realistic with deadlines.

-STEP THREE-

WEAPONS OF MASS DISTINCTION

10

CONTENT TYPES

"Success is not final, failure is not fatal:

it is the courage to continue that counts."

Sir Winston Churchill

Brace yourself. It's time for some more home truths!

There is too much content out there. Consumers are slowly being overwhelmed with the volume of content being produced on almost any given topic. In fact, according to Content Marketing Institute[19] and Marketing Profs[60] research, only 42% of organisations using content marketing feel it is having any impact. This is partly because only 44% of these brands have a content marketing strategy in place and, as a consequence, are not using the most effective content types at the right points.

The content type we choose is the vehicle for our message, so we need to be certain it is the most appropriate for our audience at the stage in the journey we're targeting. What did our research tell us about the content formats our target audience will be most receptive to?

We'll now take a closer look at some of the most effective content weapons in our battery.

BLOGS

Blogs are the hub of most brands' content marketing activities, partly because their natural structure (heading, main body, lists and links) means they can easily be optimised for search engines.

Regularly posting useful, interesting or entertaining blogs can also help us to get to know our audience better, as well as test out new topics and themes by monitoring interactions and analytics.

Our blog posts should be primarily published to owned channels, such as our website, microsites or dedicated blog sites. Publishing blog posts primarily on rented channels like LinkedIn and blog communities leaves our content at the mercy of third parties, who have the power to change rules around publishing privileges and organic reach.

ORIGINAL DATA & RESEARCH

Reports, data sheets and research studies can be extremely valuable content, particularly in B2B settings. We can either conduct a dedicated study in a targeted area of interest, or we can use data we already have that comes from our market research, customer questionnaires or general business activities.

Depending on whether the depth and volume of research justifies it, we can gear this kind of content for lead generation at the point of access (for example, by requesting contact details). We can then use this to feed more relevant content to the user in the future.

SLIDESHARE PRESENTATIONS

Using SlideShare[94], we can create and share presentations, infographics, documents, videos, PDFs, and webinars. Our content can then easily be shared across social media and embedded within websites and blogs. This is particularly good for reusing existing company presentations and materials.

GUIDES & MANUALS

Creating user guides and manuals is a great way of using in-house expertise to provide value to our target customers. Our guides don't just have to focus on how to use our products and services; they can also cover things like improving efficiency, making the most of specific features and maximising product lifespan. We can even go beyond our products and services and create guides that deal with customer 'pain points' that don't directly relate to our commercial offering.

WHITE PAPERS

In publishing a white paper, we have an opportunity to offer an authoritative perspective on specific issues in a report format. The aims of our white paper should be to help customers to understand key issues, solve a problem, or make a decision.

DATA SHEETS

Data sheets, otherwise known as technical summaries or specifications, are documents that summarise the performance and technical characteristics of services and products (such as machines and components). Publishing this kind of content alongside our products and services can help our customers to make more informed decisions throughout the buyer's journey, from the 'Purchase' to 'Advocate and Reconvert' stages.

LISTS

People love lists. How many times have you read things like *"The Top 100 X"* or *"7 reasons to Y"*? If we target our customers effectively, this kind of content can be extremely engaging and shareable, yet it doesn't always involve a huge investment in time, resources or skills. If we were a travel company, how difficult would it be for us to produce a list of our top 10 recommended holiday destinations?

LINK PAGES

Similarly to list pages, link pages pull together resources from around the internet (which can be ours or third-party) and display them in one place as a directory.

Production-wise, the main investment will be time for research and long-term maintenance of external links (which tend to move or break over time). If we work the maintenance into our content calendar, we can more easily mitigate the risk of broken links.

WEBINARS

Online seminars are a great way to provide valuable content in the form of live training, workshops, lectures and consultations. Webinar services enable real-time point-to-point communications and multicast communications from one sender to many receivers. They offer data streams of text-based messages, voice and video chat to be shared simultaneously, across the globe.

There are a number of free and paid webinar services, including Click Webinar[15] and Any Meeting[4].

EBOOKS

One of the best ways we can elevate our authority and credibility in our field is to publish an eBook. It is also one of the best ways to reach large volumes of the target audience, but our success will ultimately depend on the production quality and value of our content.

We can publish eBooks as downloads on our website, or make them accessible for Kindle and e-reader devices, using services such as Create Space[23] and Book Baby[8].

VIDEOS

Whether our content is informative, entertaining or thought provoking, video is one of the most popular and versatile content types we can choose. In terms of reach and shareability, it can offer substantial return on investment when targeted and amplified appropriately.

When it comes to publishing, there is a range of paid and free distribution channels that allow us to embed videos within websites and also enable them to be shared easily across social media channels. As a starting point, take a look at YouTube[119], Vimeo[113] and uploads direct to Facebook.

SCREENCASTS

Also known as video screen captures, screencasts are digital recordings of computer screen outputs and usually include audio narration and text annotations. They are ideal for educational uses, including software presentations, tutorials and troubleshooting guides.

There is a range of free and paid software packages we can use to create screencasts easily. Start by looking at Cam Studio[12] and Screencast-O-Matic[90].

LIVE-STREAMING VIDEO

A great way of engaging audiences with real-time content is live-streaming video. This can be used effectively for coverage of things like round-table discussions, events and presentations. Incorporate this with live audience participation, such as real-time questions and answers, and we have a truly real-time content experience.

Take a look at YouTube's live streaming service[118] and Meerkat[63].

PODCASTS

Podcasts are a great way of getting our content to target customers in an easily accessible format, which they can listen to while on the move. They tend to work best as part of a series, or at least as a consistent flow of episodes. The great thing about podcasts is they can be audio versions of written content or they can be specially produced for audio. They work great in radio programme format for discussions and interviews.

A good quality microphone and suitable recording location are paramount considerations for media quality, but it need not cost the earth. A decent USB condenser microphone can be sought from as little as $80.

INFOGRAPHICS

Infographics are great for conveying information in an easy-to-digest format with a mixture of graphics and text. Whether we're displaying processes, timelines or complex data we can use infographics to display the information simply and clearly, with easy emphasis on trends and patterns. Educational and great for social sharing, infographics can be used repeatedly by us and by other content curators.

To create an infographic, we can either use the services of a graphic designer or use an online tool like Infogram[48] or Piktochart[75].

COMICS & CARTOON STRIPS

Useful when making both simple and complex points, comic strips and cartoons are visually appealing, easy to follow and can be used to make points quickly. They can be used to demonstrate and simplify processes, explain or emphasise theories, and create humorous interpretations that our audience can identify with. If well produced, cartoons can be highly engaging and extremely sharable online.

There are a number of free and subscription online programmes that can be used to create and share this kind of content in a variety of styles, with little design experience required. Try Pixton[77] or Go Animate[35].

MEMES

Often used to represent concepts, catchphrases or pieces of media, memes use images, videos, hyperlinks, hashtags and/or pieces of text. They are very short, humorous in nature and built for sharing across social networks.

Memes are simple to make with basic editing software, but there are also a number of websites and apps that can be used, including Imgflip[46] and Meme Generator[64].

CASE STUDIES

Case studies are a great way of showing off examples of our brand at its best, along with demonstrating real-life examples of service excellence. Rather than telling our audience how great we are, we are showing them with examples they can relate to.

INTERVIEWS

Interviews with influencers, industry experts, customers and even staff within our own company can prove to be very engaging content. We can present this content in a range of formats, including copy, audio, video and in-person events.

IN-PERSON EVENTS

Great for pulling in a captive audience, hosting in-person events, such as conferences and workshops, can be particularly engaging for customers.

The keys to a successful event are a well-targeted audience, engaging promotional hooks (including topics and guest speakers) and content that is highly-relevant to the audience.

DOWNLOADABLE TEMPLATES

Creating usable templates that customers can use to complete or structure tasks is a simple and effective way of offering value. Whether it is an excel spreadsheet for bookkeeping or a dress making pattern, this type of content enables us to share existing internal resources, materials or documentation to provide value that our customers will use time and time again.

FREE STOCK

Perhaps we have a whole bank of photography or video that our target customers would find useful. By creating a database of free photography or video we can deliver value in the form of free, reusable stock media. Take a look at free image website, Unsplash[112], for inspiration.

EMAILS

We're probably already using emails to deliver marketing messages to our target customers, but we can also use this channel to deliver valuable content to our audience in the same way. We can either embed the content into email templates or link to content that lives elsewhere.

NEWS ARTICLES

Publishing new articles is a great way of demonstrating that our finger is on the pulse of our industry. By producing and/or curating relevant news articles on the topics that matter to our customers, we can take a step towards being the go-to source for news in our field. Before we commit to publishing news, we need to consider how this fits in with our long-term plan. As the name suggests, news will need to be published regularly at consistent intervals.

We can either create our own online or offline newsletter, or use an online platform, such as Paper.li[72] or The Tweeted Times[104].

THIRD-PARTY PRODUCT REVIEWS

Reviewing products and services that are relevant to our target audience can help to demonstrate our specialist expertise. But in order for our reviews to be valuable, they must be neutral and objective. For this reason, avoid reviewing products we have a commercial interest in.

On the other hand, feel free to share or republish the best and most interesting third-party reviews of our own products or services if our customers will find them useful.

CONTENT COMPETITIONS

By developing content competitions, we can attract and engage specific customer segments, build our brand profile and develop long-term relationships with our audience. Not least, they also generate a whole bank of customer-generated content.

There is a range of platforms we can use to both run the competitions and accept the entries, including social media channels (Instagram[49] and Facebook are particularly popular platforms for competitions), email communications and, of course, via our website.

Remember to include rules, terms and conditions, closing date and details of any prizes on offer.

MOBILE APPS

Mobile apps are natural born engagement tools and enable a participatory element to our content that isn't always functionally or logistically possible on other platforms.

By creating a mobile app, we can send a regular stream of valuable content straight to the hands of our target audience in a highly-targeted way. We know exactly who the user is and how they are interacting with our content. We can use this information to customise the brand experience for each customer, delivering truly valuable content at all of the crucial times.

BRANDED MICROSITES

By creating a branded microsite, we can pull together all of the content we have created for a specific theme and present it in one place under a dedicated brand. Not only does this provide us with a platform for promoting and showcasing niche content, we're able to create a more objective magazine-style feel to the package.

PRINT MAGAZINES

Though we're deep into the digital age, there is certainly still a welcome place for print magazines and pamphlets. Depending on our niche and the customers we're targeting, a print magazine might be a smart way to tap into our audience. Look at the continued success of print publications like *The Furrow* magazine, *LEGO Club* and *BenchMark Magazine*.

TV & RADIO SHOWS

While this might seem like a far-fetched idea on the face of it, many businesses and individuals build their public profiles by appearing on TV and radio shows. Whether we're aiming to star in our own network TV show like *Million Dollar Listing*, or we want to be the local radio station's go-to expert on our specialist topic, TV and radio appearance can elevate our authority faster than any other medium.

Look out for media opportunities advertised in the press, but also get in touch with TV and radio companies to offer your services as expert commentators. At the same time, get on the media radar by actively participating in relevant radio phone-ins and TV debates.

TV and radio are areas that niche targeting is less important in the grand scheme. In this case, the bigger the platform, the more celebrated our expertise.

BOOK REVIEWS

Even if we don't have the time or the resources to produce our own print book or eBook, we can still dip our toe into the world of publishing by writing book reviews. Writing a critical review of a book can demonstrate our expertise and authority in the field, while also proving we're up to date with current literature in the field.

Bear in mind that publishing our review on a bookstore website (such as Amazon) will restrict us in terms of copy length and structure, as well as reach or virality. Instead, try publishing it somewhere that offers more control, such as our own website, blog or YouTube.

*   *   *

Every business has a finite amount of money and resources to spend on marketing, so don't waste any of it by creating content types that won't earn their keep. Choosing between content types will be much easier if we allow our market research, buyer personas and buyer's journey to guide us. But, remember that the best solution might not be the most obvious.

Throw away any assumptions that tie content types to certain content ideas. For instance, just because it's a tutorial, it doesn't mean it has to be a video; just because it's a piece of analysis, it doesn't mean it has to be a whitepaper.

If you want to make a real difference in your customers' world, don't allow your messages to be constrained by archetypal content types.

So far, you have gathered all of the information you'll need to make the right decisions. Now it's time for you to make some bold judgements.

REVOLUTIONARY DIRECTIVES

1. Let the objectives for each piece of work dictate the most suitable content types.
2. Forecast the return on investment for each content type per idea.
3. Identify which content types will be most suitable for generating social media engagement and sharing.

11

STYLE GUIDE

"Trust is built with consistency."

Lincoln Chafee

I spent a number of years working as a business journalist, providing white-labelled news articles and features for a variety of companies, including banks, insurance companies and SMEs. All of the content was re-branded and published by the clients as if they had produced it themselves, so it was important that every piece was written in their own house style.

Whenever content comes from more than one producer, whether they are external providers or in-house staff, it is crucial that everyone follows the same style rules. Without uniformity in language, style and tone, the content portfolio has no consistent identity.

Remember that one of the main reasons we're creating content is to establish a distinguished voice in our field and tie the great content we produce to our brand. But how do we do that without banging on about our brand within the content?

By developing a style guide, we can create a coherent brand image that our customers will more easily recognise as ours. The standards we set will become our calling card identifiers and help to create more consistent, polished and professional experiences for our audience. The more consistent we are, the more likely it is that people will see what makes us special.

If we don't already have a set of documented guidelines in place, we need to establish some before we start creating anything.

Our style guide should cover information about brand rules and editorial principles, such as tone and voice.

OUR BRAND RULES

Our brand identity separates us from our competitors, so it's important that we affirm how those distinguishing features are reflected in the content we publish. Within the brand section of our guide, we need to address the following:

1. **Use of company name:** Some companies can be referred to in a variety of ways, for instance using acronyms or shortened versions, i.e. BA for British Airways. We need to specify how our company will be referred to in various situations. For example, perhaps on Twitter we will use an abbreviated version, but on the company blog site use the full name?

2. **Use of our straplines:** If we use any tagline, straplines, or company mottos, in what situations are these appropriate? Do we have different strap lines for specific scenarios or publishing channels?

3. **Logo no-nos:** Most companies have rules around how their logo should be used, including size, how much space should be around it on print and online and what kind of imagery it can be placed alongside. What are our stipulations?

4. **Colours:** What are the brand colours and how should they be used? Are there any variations? Recommend some colour combinations and outline any that should be avoided.

5. **Typography:** What specific font and lettering styles are acceptable and does this depend on channel? Some fonts are designed for use online and don't work as well in print, so we may need online and offline variations. For example, at Group Dane, we...

use this font online

and this font offline.

6. **Images:** Some businesses have a collection of images or a specific image aligned with their brand. Do we have a specific set or type of images that should be used in certain situations?

EDITORIAL PRINCIPLES

Don't be tempted to go overboard with editorial rules just for the sake of it, but a solid set of general, concise principles will help us to standardise things like:

1. **Vocabulary:** Define preferred use of variations like 'while' or 'whilst' and 'among' or 'amongst'.

2. **Punctuation:** Specify a standard use of things like colons and semicolons, exclamation marks, hyphens and dashes.

3. **Acronyms and abbreviations:** Provide guidance on whether we should spell out the component words the first time we use it, every time or never.

4. **Terms to avoid:** Are there any specific words or phrases we should refrain from using? Depending on our product area and audience, we may need to provide guidelines on when technical or specialist language is and isn't appropriate.

5. **Fluffy words:** Are there any special words we want to link to specific topics? For example, an energy company might want to tie the brand to words like 'comfy', 'toasty', 'snuggly'.

6. **Capitalisation:** Do we want to use uppercase, title case or sentence case for things like headings and product or service names?

7. **Dates and times:** Specify what formats we should use for dates, such as day/month/year or month/day/year, along with whether or not to use 'th' (e.g. 6th June or 6 June). How do we want to present times, will it be 12pm, 12:00 or noon?

8. **Numbers:** Will we use numerals or words, or a mixture? For example, some style guides stipulate numbers 1-10 as numerals and from eleven onwards as words.

9. **Symbols:** Specify when we should use symbols or words (e.g. 100% or 100 percent, 30° or 30 degrees, etc.).

10. **Words to hyphenate:** How do we want to deal with hyphens to connect words and word elements (e.g. e-mail or email, e-commerce or ecommerce, etc.).

11. **Specific word variations:** How should certain words be connected or separated? List common examples relevant to our field (e.g. web site or website, white paper or whitepaper).

12. **Hyperlinks:** When we link to other webpages online, should we write the full URL, drop the WWWs or use link text (e.g. http://www.bbc.co.uk, bbc.co.uk or <u>BBC</u>)?

TONE

It is important that our guide indicates the appropriate tone for various situations. Our content is our brand's voice, so how do we want it to sound and what personality traits should it convey?

1. **Formality:** Would our audience be receptive to a more formal or less formal tone in certain situations?

2. **First, second or third:** We need to specify in what situations we should use first-person (I, we), second-person (you, your) or third-person (he/she, they) personal pronouns in our content.

3. **Principles and personality:** What is our brand's personality and how will we convey this through tone of voice? For example, are we aiming for friendly, inspiring and helpful, or do we want to come across as edgy, sassy and confident?

4. **Tone no-nos:** Just as it's important to specify the personality traits we want to express, we also need to outline any undesirable ones. For example, are we to avoid anything that comes across as overly official, smug or glib?

SHOW, DON'T JUST TELL

The main problem with describing our brand's tone of voice using personality traits is that they are, of course, subjective. For instance, my definition of 'jolly and approachable' is probably completely different to yours.

Therefore, it's important to illustrate our points with clear examples. Always aim to use real-world scenarios relevant to the content types we're going to be publishing. Along with our examples, it might be useful to sprinkle the guide with notes explaining our rationale.

AUDIENCE

So far, we have talked at length about keeping our audience central to everything we produce, so it's only natural that this should also be reflected in our style guide.

By keeping our buyer personas and the buyer's journey to hand, we can build in guidelines that support different audience requirements. If necessary, we can specify a slightly different tone when we're targeting certain customer segments. For example, when I was online communications manager at a utility company, we adopted highly-distinct styles when communicating with home customers and corporate audiences.

What tone and style will our buyer personas be most receptive to?

COMMUNICATE AND UPHOLD

Once we have developed our style guide, we need to make sure all of our content producers fully understand it and are committed to upholding its values. I've found that presenting the guide and discussing its features with content producers in-person encourages the fastest, most positive implementation.

EVOLUTION

The best style guides are living documents that evolve and develop over time. It's important that we listen to feedback, monitor how our audience interacts with the content and fine tune the guide over time. Every new iteration will be stronger and more aligned to our target audience.

*   *   *

Think of every contact a customer has with your brand as the most important encounter of your life.

But, the obvious problem is, most of the time you are not going to be present to do the talking. Instead, you're going to be communicating through a piece of content, which may not have even been created by you. Are you going to allow a dissident voice to speak on your behalf, or will you make sure everything you publish sounds like it has come from your own lips? Think of the style guide as a briefing for your brand's delegated spokesperson.

Ultimately, we're aiming to develop a comfortable and familiar personification of our brand through consistency and good practice. By creating and upholding our style guide, no matter who produces our content, it will resonate with our brand values.

Remember, the style guide is our most loyal brand protector.

REVOLUTIONARY DIRECTIVES

1. Establish brand and style rules with your buyer personas in mind.
2. Consider editorial and brand variations for different channels.
3. Uphold, but be willing to evolve and refine the guide over time.

12

DRIVING QUALITY

"Quality is not an act, it is a habit."

Aristotle

Every day for work, I wear a suit and tie with a folded pocket square. Over the last few years, this has become my trademark among people that know me. But, for me, it isn't just a style choice – when I'm wearing these clothes, I feel like I'm ready to take on anything that comes my way. Batman has his cowl, Superman has his cape and I have my pocket square!

The way we present ourselves, sends out a clear message to the world. What do you want that message to be? For me, it is about demonstrating effort, professionalism and attentiveness. Whether I'm meeting clients, colleagues or rivals, I want them to know I'm there with full commitment and strong conviction. Have you heard of the expression "The clothes maketh the man"?

Whether we are meeting customers at the cash register or speaking with them through our content, the way we present ourselves will dramatically influence perceptions of our brand.

I'm not suggesting we make all of our content overly formal like my clothes, but we do need to let an air of quality and reliability permeate everything we do.

VOLUME & VELOCITY RISKS

It's easy to get carried away with the idea of filling space and pumping out masses of content in all different formats, across a range of platforms. But, the more content we are producing at pace, the more quality and consistency comes under threat, particularly if we're stretching limited resources.

Consider the 'Speed – Quality – Cost Triangle'. For every piece of content we create, there is a trade-off between the speed we can deliver it, the production cost and the quality of the end result. It's not possible to have more than two of these factors working in our favour at any one time. For example, if we're looking to deliver the content quickly to a high quality, it will be expensive to produce; if we want it to be high quality and inexpensive to produce, it will not be delivered quickly. The final option is the one we're to avoid at all costs: delivering quickly, but inexpensively – this is where quality fails.

Figure 9: *Speed – Quality – Cost Triangle*

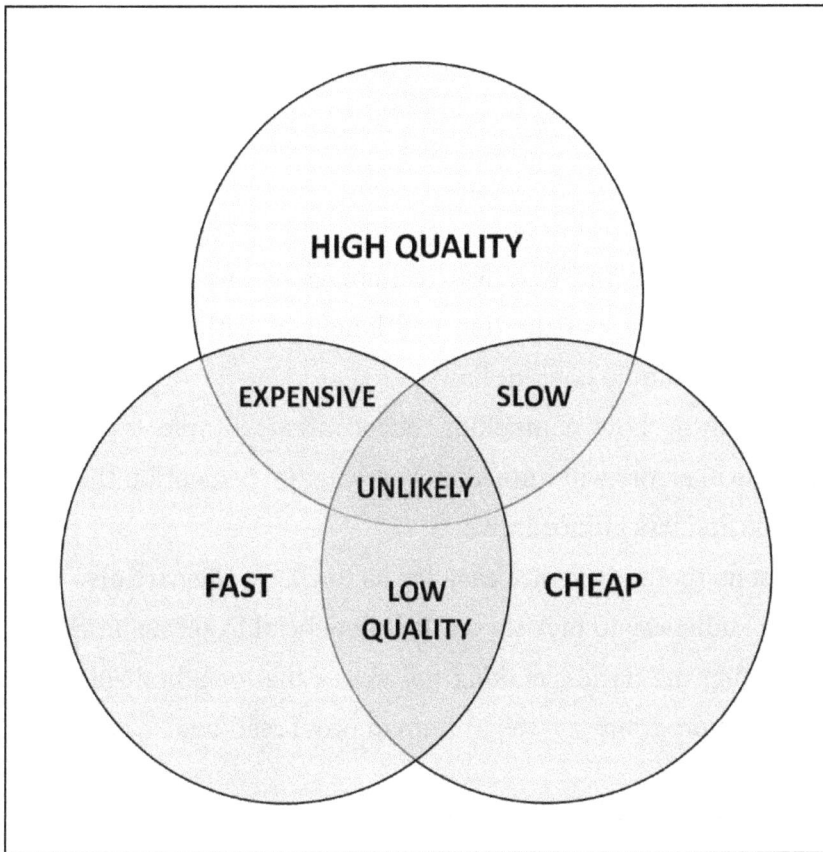

Problems with our content reflect badly on our brand; if customers spot quality flaws, they will expect the same sloppy effort from us when it comes to our products and services.

We can mitigate these risks by complementing our style guide with a quality assurance framework that all work must pass through before it is published.

The process can be as simple as a manual checklist, or it can involve automated devices or sophisticated checking systems. In all cases, there are some crucial factors to consider before we hit the little red publish button.

COPY 101

The most obvious and easy way to manage quality checks are for spelling, grammar, punctuation and language, yet these are some of the most common content flaws.

No matter how compelling our content, simple typos and grammatical errors will immediately create the perception that it is low value and less authoritative.

Just as these errors are easy for us to check, they are also very easy for audiences to pick up on. It is beneficial to set up a process for checking the basics, making full use of the tools built-into our text editing programs as well as human proof reading.

APPROPRIATE MULTIMEDIA

Multimedia like videos, slideshows, photos, playlists, audio and photography can be highly engaging, but only if it is produced to an appropriate quality.

We might not need every piece of content to be top notch, but we do need to make a judgement call on whether or not the media is appropriate quality for the context it's used and the target audience.

As we discussed earlier, lower-quality multimedia might be acceptable if it's user-generated, deliberately 'home-made', or it fits into the context of its channel, such as Vine or Periscope. But in some cases, the context of the content will call for higher, even professional quality media. For example, if we're recording a podcast series, we're probably going to want the content to be as professional as possible.

One aspect we can never compromise on, however, is the quality of the message. Whatever context, regardless of the audience, the message is the purpose of the content. What do we want it to say? What statement do we want to make? Is this clear enough?

GRAPHIC DESIGN

When producing anything that has a visual element, use a professional graphic designer or the best in-house resource. Whether it's a flyer, an infographic or a web element, try and not be tempted to do it without the right skills or experience. Not only will an inferior attempt be less likely to get used or shared, there is also a chance it will damage perceptions of our brand. Is our business slapdash, unprofessional or dated like that homemade infographic?

LAYOUT

The layout of the content will affect its usability, so we must ensure we deliver the best possible experience by presenting the content in a logical format. Huge blocks of text are difficult to negotiate, especially online, and could cause your audience to skim read.

If we are not thinking about our audience's needs when creating our content, they simply will not use it.

DON'T GET STUFFED (WITH KEYWORDS)

Let's acknowledge for a moment that we have an ulterior motive at play. Although we're working really hard to create content that our audiences will find useful, interesting or entertaining, we are doing this because we want something: a place in our target customers' minds.

Naturally, in our quest to get our content out there to as many of the right people as possible, we'll want to search engine optimise it with relevant keywords. But be careful not to diminish the overall quality and readability of the piece with unnatural keyword stuffing or phrase manipulation. Our audience won't like it and, actually, neither will the search engines.

*   *   *

Your brand may not be the biggest or most influential in the marketplace, but what makes you the *BEST* in your niche area? Is it your unique relationship with customers? Or, perhaps your passion for the topic? Whatever the proposition, the clarity of your voice and the quality of its delivery will define your customers' perceptions.

Next time you're about to hit the publish button, stop for a moment. How much do you believe in this piece of content? Do you genuinely see where it delivers value? Don't allow things like the pressures of a publishing schedule or a rapidly emerging opportunity to cloud your judgement. Quality concerns should trump all other commitments!

Remember, delivering quality content is your obligation, your privilege, your raison d'être.

REVOLUTIONARY DIRECTIVES

1. Create and share a quality assurance checklist.

2. Iteratively update and improve content based on feedback.

3. Ensure amplification tactics (e.g. search engine optimisation and viral tactics) don't breach quality standards.

13

CONTENT CURATION

"All knowledge is connected to all other knowledge.
The fun is in making the connections."

Arthur Aufderheide

When most of us think about the websites Huffington Post and BuzzFeed, we think of interesting and entertaining articles. We might also remember one or two particular articles we have enjoyed recently. But it doesn't occur to most people that a lot of this content isn't actually produced by these publishers.

Rather than creating all of the content in-house, these brands (and thousands of others like them) spend a lot of time sourcing third-party content that they believe the audience will be interested in.

For both of these publishers, the curation process is quite

simple. It involves carefully sourcing suitable content, adding a niche headline, contextualising it with a short introduction, slotting in the original content and referencing to the original author.

Beth Kanter, co-author of *Measuring the Networked Non-Profit*, provides a useful description of the content curation process: "Content curation is the process of sorting through the vast amounts of content on the web and presenting it in a meaningful and organised way around a specific theme. The work involves sifting, sorting, arranging, and publishing information. A content curator cherry picks the best content that is important and relevant to share with their community."

Republishing other people's content is a great way to use their voice and influence to help bolster our messages, deliver value to our customers and drive forward our strategy by supporting specific objectives. The practice can not only add strength and credibility to our messages by demonstrating objectivity, it also means we're able to provide our audience with great quality content without having to create it all ourselves.

By sifting, sorting and republishing the best of the information available in our category, we're able to position ourselves as thought leaders in our field. The fact we're making qualified editorial decisions about other people's content demonstrates ultimate knowledge in the field. Plus, from our audience's point of view, we are saving them time by finding, filtering and organising content that they want to see.

In fact, from a practical point of view, content curation can help us to beat the top challenges we face as content marketers, including saving time and money and ensuring a steady flow of engaging multi-format content.

Figure 10: Top five cited content marketing challenges

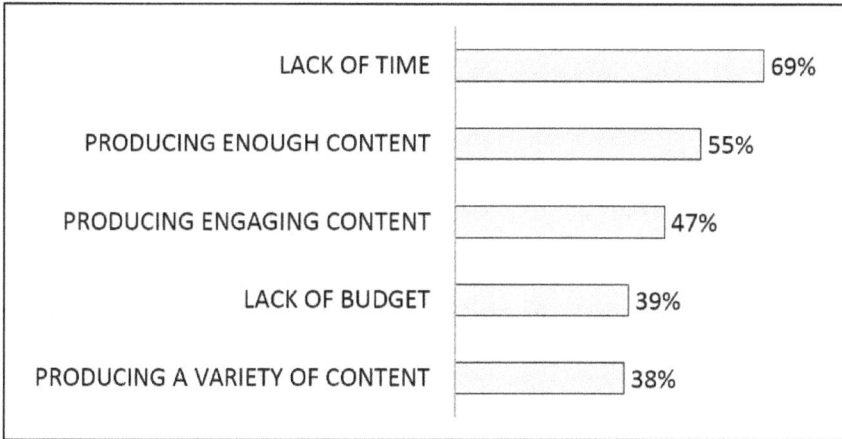

Data source: 2014 B2B Content Marketing Trends North America © Content Marketing Institute/Marketing Profs

Given the benefits, it's no surprise that 82% of marketers are publishing curated content (according to IMN Content Marketing Survey[47]), with 48% curating at least once a week (source: Curata[24]).

Although the advantages of effective content curation are clear, there are a number of things we need to consider in order to protect our brand and mitigate some of the risks that come with using other people's content.

EDITORIAL JUDGEMENT

Too many content marketers go crazy with curation because they see it as an easy and cost-effective way to flood their market with content. There are a number of tools available that make it very easy to gather and republish content from around the internet (we will look at tools later), but selecting the right content to publish requires skill and close consideration of our objectives.

If we publish content that isn't perfectly in tune with our target audience and our objectives, we risk portraying our brand as out of touch and irrelevant. Content with the wrong focus will only dilute our message and distract our audience from the really valuable stuff in our portfolio.

The same principles we use to make editorial judgements when we're creating content also apply to the curation process. Is the content highly-relevant to our target customers? How does the content help support the buyer's journey? What particular goals or objectives does it support?

LISTEN, WATCH, READ

We need to cast our net as widely as possible in order to find the best content relevant to our target audience and objectives. There are a number of tools that can alert us to content that is being published within our areas of interest, including:

- Curata[24] gathers topic-specific content from hundreds of thousands of sources across the internet. With a high degree of tailoring, the system learns and dynamically adapts to content preferences and easily integrates with CMS (content management systems), social and email marketing platforms. This is the heavyweight curator's choice, with 'Professional' and 'Enterprise' monthly pricing options.

- ScoopIt[87] uses big data semantic technology to scour 20 million web pages each day for high-quality, relevant content. This system comes with the Smart Calendar to help plan and manage the publishing process. There are a range of packages from a free taster option to an enterprise-level 'content director' plan.

- Swayy[100] helps us to discover and reuse engaging content across social media. With a built-in analytics platform, the system is designed to suggest the most effective content for growing our community. Prices range from a free basic account to a 100 dashboard agency-level plan.

- Feedley[31] compiles news feeds from a wide range of sources and includes an easy customisation and publishing dashboard. The generous basic package is free with premium upgrades to Pro and Team versions available.

- TrapIt[108] use advanced artificial intelligence and machine learning to create real-time content collections, called 'traps,' The system, which allows drill-down by location and media type, can publish content to websites, social media and mobile applications. A free demo version is available upon request.

SUPPORTING THEMES

Think of our curated material as nominees for Best Supporting Actor, while our own content takes the leading roles. We need to ensure that everything we collect fits in with our broader themes of focus. How can third-party content create a more rounded picture and contribute to shaping our topics? If it's not obvious how the content supports our specific messages, we probably shouldn't be publishing it.

REINFORCE OUR VOICE

Let's step outside of our own world for a moment and remember that our audience probably isn't interested in our brand per se. They are interested in meeting some kind of need and nothing more.

The problem is, everything we produce ourselves is quietly whispering "me, me, me". Naturally, our content is all about *our* advice and *our* perspective, but too much of our own messaging without support from objective third parties starts to give our content a narcissistic feel.

We can balance our "me, me, me" voice by using third-party content to demonstrate support for the content we are putting out. We should look for content that we can use to validate and reinforce our own voice.

GO FOR INFLUENCERS

Have you the heard the expression "You are the company you keep"? It is certainly true that customers will judge us against the people we're associated with. Just think about the millions of dollars companies pay to be endorsed by celebrities and sport personalities.

By curating the content of key influencers in our field, we can link our brand with the key individuals and organisations our customers care about. Publishing influencer content not only demonstrates positive affinities, it also allows us to borrow some of their authority.

CREATE A BUZZ

Curation can help us to highlight the discussions people are having about the quieter topic areas we're interested in. We won't whip up much interest in a new niche area if we're the only people talking about it. Let's pull all existing activity together from a variety of sources and present it together. This can reinforce the importance of the topic and attract more attention to it, creating a niche topical buzz.

To add some more credibility to the topic we want to highlight, it is a good idea to pepper it with content from contributors that don't have a commercial interest in the field, such as commentators and independent bloggers.

FIND HARMONIOUS AGENDAS

By identifying publishers that we can have a mutually beneficial relationship with, we can create content partnerships with other brands to bolster our provision. This reduces our resourcing requirements and potentially increases our reach by exposing our content to their audience.

But, remember, regardless of any content sharing deal, all of the same rules apply to editorial decisions; we will only curate content that is appropriate quality and most relevant to our audience.

PLUGGING GAPS

What are the gaps in our expertise or resources that prevent us from creating certain types of content? By curating content that specifically fits into areas we need to prop up, we can provide our target customers with everything they could possibly need.

As well as adding value, our audience will begin to recognise us as a source of objective content on the hot topics. We want to become the go-to source for carefully filtered content.

SUPPORTING SNIPPETS

How can we use snippets of other peoples content to support our created content? Bolstering our created content with occasional gems of curated material will save us time and strengthen our arguments.

LEGAL CONSIDERATIONS

Whenever we're using someone else's content within our own work, there are potential legal risks.

Pawan Deshpande, Founder and CEO of Curata, explains: "Fair-use and curation of other people's content becomes an issue when it's not handled properly because the interest of the curator and the publisher overlap significantly. They both want a piece of the same pie: site traffic, increased SEO and visitor retention.

"When the curation is done wrong, the curator's interests are served but the publisher sees no benefit. But if it's done properly, in a symbiotic manner that makes it a win-win, curation can serve the interest of the publisher, and curator, and ultimately the audience."

Figure 11: Publisher and creator overlap

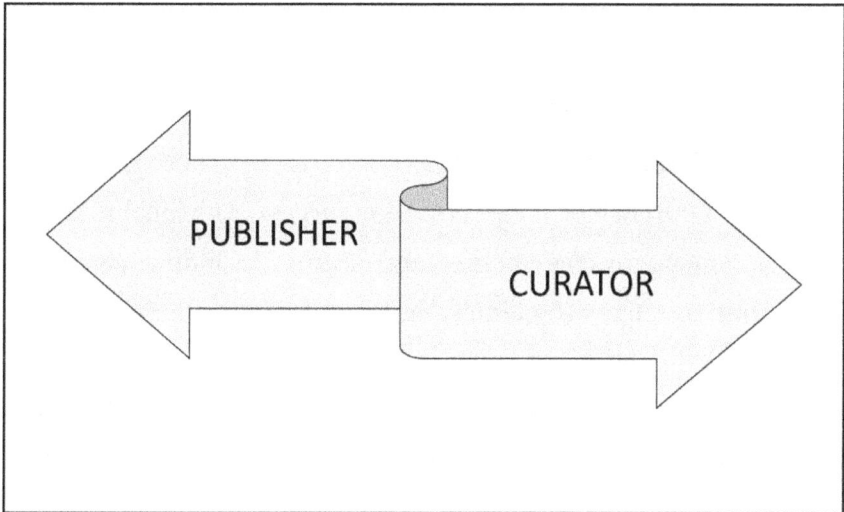

Kimberley Isbell, of the Nieman Journalism Lab, studied a Harvard Law report to develop an extensive set of best practice recommendations. In a nutshell, here are the top five best practices:

1. Only reproduce portions of the content required to make a specific point; don't reproduce the whole piece.
2. Don't curate the majority of our content from the same source.
3. Clearly identify the source and author of the content.
4. Link to the original source, wherever possible.
5. Explain why we are using the content by introducing and contextualising the content.

THE RIGHT MIX

There is a lot of debate around how much of our content should be created versus curated. Some businesses run with 80-100% curated, while others don't curate content at all. There is no one-size-fits-all approach or ideal recipe for success. The ideal ratio for use will depend on the market and sector (including customer needs), our resources (including the size of our business) and our objectives. What do we need to do in order to drive us forward towards the big aim? In all cases, we need to make sure all of our content is effectively moving customers through the buyer's journey.

*   *   *

The revolution will be no picnic.

At times, our efforts to secure a place at the top of our market will feel like a bloody battle. Yet, the biggest challenges we face won't always come in the form of direct hits from business rivals.

The weakest elements of our own offering, like gaps in expertise and resources, could seriously affect our credibility on certain topics. Occasionally, we're going to need to call in some back-up.

These reinforcements may come in the form of third-party content, carefully curated to bolster these weaker areas. By making smart editorial decisions, we can sort and contextualise valuable content on behalf of our audience. In this case, the value comes in the form of the content package we have created rather than the component pieces.

We can ramp up our clout by linking in with publishers to develop a mutually beneficial relationship. To paraphrase Lyndon B. Johnson, it is better to have certain people inside our tent "spitting" out than outside our tent "spitting" in.

Don't wait for shots to be fired before you identify where your back up is coming from.

REVOLUTIONARY DIRECTIVES

1. Carefully cherry-pick third-party content that will help to support your own big aims, goals or objectives.
2. Contextualise curated content within key topics or themes.
3. Only use curated content if it is beneficial for you and the original publisher.

14

REAL-TIME PUBLISHING

"The time is now, the place is here."

Dan Millman

Soon after leaving university, I was lucky enough to land a role as a journalist for a business services company.

I had graduated with a degree in English Language and Literature and had been writing stories, plays and poems for almost as long as I could remember, so I was quite confident in my abilities. Yet, each day, I dreaded the 4 o'clock post mortem. This was the time that the whole team would stop what they were doing and proofread each other's work. I was never satisfied that my articles were 100% finished, but I would begrudgingly print them off and hand them to my boss, Chloie. I would then sit and listen for the sound of her pen scratching her corrections onto the warm, printer-fresh paper. Did I put enough emphasis on X? Should I have covered Y? It was torture.

After about two months, I mentioned my agony to Chloie. She said something to me that completely and permanently changed my outlook, "By the time you're 100% happy, the story will no longer be news."

Chloie was right (she usually was). By hanging on too long for perfection, we risk reducing the impact and relevance of our content. Nevertheless, I've noticed the same trait in most of the content creators that I have worked with since. These concerns seem to affect all creative people to some degree, from copywriters to graphic designers, from illustrators to videographers. If we want to publish our content at the height of its relevance, we need to break this attitude.

So far, we have discussed how important planning is to our content marketing activities, but remember that the world we operate in is an unpredictable place: economies are fragile, markets can change rapidly and customer segments can appear and disappear in the blink of an eye. Sometimes the only way we can seize unexpected opportunities and swerve dips in the road is to adapt and respond quickly, if not instantly. What does this mean for our content activities?

We can react to real-time developments in our market and seize time-limited opportunities by publishing certain types of content on-the-fly. Reacting and adapting to the audience's world can make our voice more relevant and dynamic, but it can be a risky tactic, so we need to get it right.

IDENTIFY KEY CONVERSATIONS

What are the topics, issues and discussions we want our brand to be associated with? They might be conversations people are already having, or they might be new ones that we're anticipating. Think about how we can valuably contribute to and fuel these conversations early on. How will this content help to bolster our voice among the target audience?

LISTEN UP

We can monitor the use of keywords and phrases related to the topics and conversations we are interested in. The best way is to use social media monitoring tools and online keyword scrapers to sift through blogs (including blog comments), news articles and other user-contributed content. There are a large amount of systems available to help with monitoring:

- For social media monitoring, my favourite system is Radian6[81]. With huge data depths, this system scours the internet and highlights virtually every relevant conversation happening right now across the social web.

- Services like BrandWatch[9] dashboard complex keyword searches across social platforms and beyond, with a high degree of filtering. Like Radian6, this is a paid option, but well worth considering if budget allows.

- The best of the free systems is probably Hootsuite, which enables us to identify the words and phrases we're interested in across various social channels, all displayed in a series of real-time feeds.

- Google Alerts is a great free service that allows us to identify keywords and phrases and get real-time alerts when they appear in news and other online publications. There is also a special setting to include results from social media sites.

PIVOT AND ADAPT CONTENT

It is important that we are ready to adapt to the market challenges and opportunities whenever necessary. Don't be afraid to bring scheduled content forward in the content calendar if it is particularly relevant to a current topic. Market need always trumps the schedule.

The same goes for archived and live content. If there is an opportunity to bring it back to prominence or reinvent it, go ahead and adapt, refocus, or republish. But be careful not to crowbar content into tenuously linked topics, as the lack of relevance will be obvious and will only devalue our voice.

PREPARING FOR INVASION

It is best to have a bank of content in reserve, specifically organised into the conversations we're interested in. When the big, important conversations are raging, we'll be armed and ready to contribute rich and valuable content.

INDIVIDUAL TARGETING

We have already discussed how important key market influencers are. While it is crucial that we listen to how they are using their dominant voices, we must remember that every single member of our audience has the potential to influence others.

Some of the biggest companies in the world, including Philips, take the time to respond and deliver bespoke content to audiences of just one person. There is no engagement like a one-to-one engagement.

Creating ad hoc content for individual customers might sound like a great deal of work, but it shouldn't actually be an indiscriminate process. In reality, it is more about responding to individual customers in a very personal way with content that will also appeal to the rest of the audience segment.

ADD VALUE OR GO HOME

Although we need to look for content marketing opportunities around the hot topics we're interested in, we don't need to interact with every single conversation and related sub-topic. Only get involved with hot topics that are relevant to our buyer personas and that we're able to add value to.

DON'T KILL CONVERSATIONS

If we see conversations on websites, social media, blogs and forums that we want to get involved with, it's important that we keep our contributions appropriate and highly-relevant. We want to position ourselves as part of the community, almost like friends sharing useful information. But, bear in mind that nobody likes that friend who won't let anyone else speak; we can be that clever, understanding and helpful friend instead.

Remember, we are not telling people where to go next or what to do, we're just going with the flow of the conversation and helping with content where it might be useful. Avoid spammy interruptions!

CREATING IN REAL-TIME

Sometimes an opportunity will arise that calls for content to be created from scratch. The scope for pay-off will be more risky because there just won't be time to follow all of the usual planning and development processes. However, there are a few questions to answer before creating anything on-the-fly, including:

1. How will the content specifically contribute to our big aim, goals or objectives?
2. Will the topic still be 'hot' by the time it is ready to publish?
3. Are there any legal considerations associated with publishing the content right now?
4. Is the situation really time-limited?

*   *   *

How committed are you to giving your customers what they need? Make it the reason for your entire existence and dedicate your time to focussing on enriching their lives with your content and, believe me, your customers will quickly notice. The more you understand them and respond to their evolving needs, the more chance you will have of earning a place in their lives.

For me, it's about heightening empathy by listening to customers' rants and sharing their joys. If you aren't watching, listening and relating to customers, they will quickly realise you are speaking *at* them, not *with* them.

Go and give it your all to position yourself as that brand that listens to customers and responds with value.

REVOLUTIONARY DIRECTIVES

1. Set up an appropriate real-time monitoring system.
2. Focus efforts on the topics and themes that matter most to your brand.
3. Add value to conversations or don't get involved.

-STEP FOUR-

STAGING YOUR COUP

15

CREATING YOUR NICHE

"If you see a bandwagon, it's too late."

James Goldsmith

A couple of years ago, Group Dane worked on a digital project with award-winning stage and screen writer, Mark Davies Markham.

I have never met anyone who tells a story in-person quite as captivatingly as Mark. With his intense eyes and a million facial expressions per minute, he knows exactly how to hold his listener's attention. Like a cross between Jack Nicholson and John Malkovich, he exudes charisma, defiance and intrigue in equal measure. He is a natural born storyteller.

Mark is perhaps best-known for his Olivier award-winning West End musical, *Taboo* (a collaboration with Boy George), along with his writing for iconic British television series' such as *EastEnders*, *Band of Gold* and *This Life*.

Though Mark has a glittering portfolio of work that has appealed to the masses, a certain volume of his work is targeted towards specific niches. For the past decade, he has written numerous drama serials for BBC Radio 4's *Women's Hour*. The BBC describes it as "the programme that offers a female perspective on the world", which isn't the obvious audience for a male writer with a background in the rough and ready eighties punk scene. So how did Mark find this niche?

There is general misconception that niches are 'discovered' but in reality, we create them by recognising our own strengths in relation to specific opportunities. One of Mark's finest skills is his ability to write hard-hitting, highly-empathetic and emotionally-provocative drama, which also happens to be some of the most popular content for BBC Radio 4's *Women's Hour*.

So how does a male writer effectively target a niche female audience? Perhaps one of the things that makes Mark's stories so compelling is the fact that he makes it his business to understand his audience inside out. Every day, he studies them, learning more about their needs, pain points and desires, which helps him to continually develop and refine his approach.

How can we learn from Mark's example and identify the best niche audiences to target? More to the point, why should we even care about appealing to niche groups when we want to maximise our income? All will become clear.

So many businesses make the mistake of trying to get their content to the biggest general audience. It doesn't make sense to invest valuable time and money in getting our message out to people that will never buy from us, let alone take any interest in our content. By focussing on a niche audience interest that matches our specialist expertise, we can achieve a better effort to return ratio.

We can start by identifying specific customer needs that are not being fully addressed (if at all) by other content producers.

COMPETITION KILLER

It doesn't matter how big our competitors are, they cannot own every niche.

It is a good idea to look at the content gaps we found during our research and home in on the ones most relevant to our knowledge and capabilities.

To this end, we're more interested in what our competitors are not doing well rather than their areas of excellence.

THE RIGHT PLATFORM

Having niche focusses is also going to help us to make better decisions about publishing platforms and channels. Rather than simply pumping out content on those we're already using, we need to be much shrewder. Where is our audience? In what format can we best deliver our specialist content? For example, would our website be the best place for a car cleaning guide, or would this be better printed on the side of a bucket? Be creative!

IDENTIFY LUCRATIVE CUSTOMER TYPES

Specifically, which of our buyer personas represents the most profitable group? We can find content niches for all of our audience groups, but the first and most important is the one that brings in the most money to our business per capita. Embedding our brand into the hearts and minds of this audience group will be the most valuable to our business.

IDENTIFY HIGHLY-SPECIFIC STRENGTHS

Imagine our business is about to sit in the chair on the TV quiz *Mastermind*. What is our specialist subject? Imagine everything depends on us pinpointing just one thing that we're the world leading expert on. Be as specific as possible, then even more so.

DEPTH OF NEED

What are our buyer personas group asking for? What do they need, specifically? How much traction is content relevant to these needs likely to get? Revisit our earlier research to identify the most common queries our customers have within our area of expertise. Your keyword data will come in particularly useful here.

*   *   *

By creating the right niche areas of focus, we're able to highlight our specialisms among the most profitable customer segments. Rather than thinly covering a broad spectrum, we should dominate the topics in which we can have the most authority. Nobody wants to be a small fish in a big pond.

We need to look deep inside our market and tease out those issues that aren't being dealt with. What are the things that our competitors just will not or cannot do?

Every single revolution in history has started with a niche following, whether it be the Bolsheviks in Russia, the slaves of Saint Domingue, or the advent of Henry Ford's motorcar. It is time to take ownership of our niche and start to pull together our own following.

REVOLUTIONARY DIRECTIVES

1. Pinpoint your most profitable audience group.
2. Identify your brand's highly-specialist strengths.
3. Investigate the depth of need within these niche topics.

16

IDEA DEVELOPMENT

"What has been will be again, what has been done
will be done again; there is nothing new
under the sun."

Ecclesiastes

As part of my research for this book, I must have read more than a hundred blog posts about coming up with ideas for new content. Most of them had titles along the lines of "10 easy content marketing ideas" and "50 content marketing ideas for your website". Quite a few interesting points were made about the ideas process and there were a couple of useful tips related to freeing the mind of clutter, but I noticed that most of the posts were missing the point.

Of the blog posts I read, at least 70% led under the misapprehension that content marketing is about creating lots of content, largely indiscriminate of focus. Freeze! Put your pen down.

As content marketers, we aren't just looking to flood the community with masses of 'stuff' – we're aiming to provide highly-relevant, valuable content that reaches our audience at the right moments. If we find ourselves trying to pluck ideas out of thin air and somehow engineer them to fit our audience, we need to stop. The ideas we come up with *must* be informed by what our audience wants or needs and nothing else.

The key to nurturing the best content ideas is knowing our target audience inside out. It's only by thinking about their needs and desires, in the context of the buyer's journey, that we'll know the difference between good and bad ideas.

It is now time to pull together all of the intelligence we've gathered so far and use this to guide and inspire our thoughts.

SWEET SPOTS

There is a wonderful point where our specialist knowledge and expertise intersects with specific customers' interests. We call this the 'sweet spot' because targeting this area will usually yield maximum returns.

Figure 12: The sweet spot

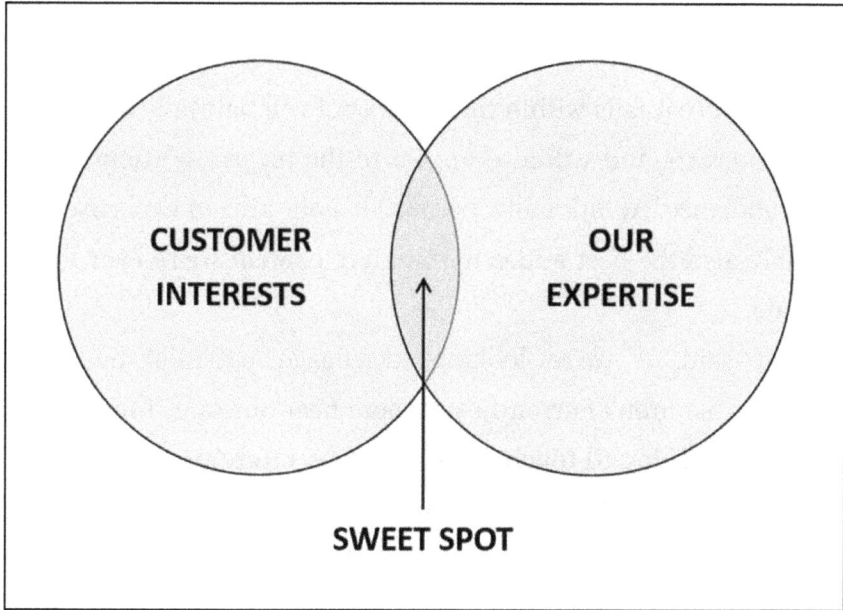

Whenever we're thinking about content ideas, we need to consider how we can use our existing cache of expertise to drill into specific customer interests.

Where is our sweet spot? Answer the following questions:

- How does our expertise address issues our audience cares about most?
- Which of our audience's priorities match our specialist subjects?
- What knowledge does our audience crave that we have in abundance?

- Which of our audience's dreams could we most easily make come true?

Content that falls within the sweet spot will naturally be easiest for us to create and will also appeal to the biggest portion of our target audience. Additionally, because it's our area of expertise, it's probably also the best authority-building content we're ever likely to create.

That said, if we're looking to engage potential audience segments that aren't currently anywhere near our sales funnel, this content isn't going to touch them. To lasso future prospects early, we need to also think outside of our comfort zone.

THINK BEYOND THE PRODUCT

If we can set our brand and products to one side for a moment, we can think about the bigger picture for our personas. What does their world look like? What are the things they care about? What are they doing with their lives right now?

Jay Baer, founder of Convince and Convert[22], talks a lot about "marketing sideways", which is basically content marketing that is inherently useful, but is not about brand or product. This approach, according to Jay, "transcends the transaction, and creates awareness for your brand at the top of the funnel – among potential customers that otherwise might not be introduced to your company and its offerings".

We need to think about content that will link us up with future prospects that we would struggle to touch with brand or product-related content. How can we capture their attention and interest?

How can we establish a relationship that will eventually lead them on to the buyer's journey?

For inspiration, look at Red Bull's focus on extreme sports and music media. This content isn't linked to the company's product at all, but it serves the brand by developing the right image among the target audience. How could this approach work for us?

PAIN POINTS

One of the best ways to attract our target audience is by appealing to their 'pain points'. We can do this by using our content to address (or even solve) specific problems, questions and direct needs.

Not only does this kind of content demonstrate relevant expertise, it also touches our target audience at a pivotal moment in the journey. It's no secret that buyers experiencing issues or 'pain' are most motivated to seek a new solution or switch brands. We can tap into that opportunity.

But how can we find out what those specific pain points are? Consider all of the behavioural information we have gathered (our *research*, the *buyer's journey* and our *buyer personas*) and answer the following questions:

- What are the main challenges our customers face?
- What are their perceived barriers to progress?
- Which issues and frustrations matter to them most?
- What do they most want to change or improve?
- What are their biggest fears?

We need to think about content ideas that address these pain points, but equally consider how important this kind of content can be to the 'Awareness and Discovery' stage of the buyer's journey. What can we do to drive the buyer forward at this early stage? Remember, the people experiencing these pain points will be more open to a new solution, so we need to make the most of our calls to action. How can we use content to form part of a chain that leads potential customers onto the buyer's journey?

EARLY BIRD ON TRENDS

The smartest content marketers make their efforts more efficient by monitoring search trends and forecast surges in activity.

Analysing web search trends can help us to see what content our target demographic is searching for now, as well as what they are likely to be looking for in the future.

When we used Google Trends as part of our research, what emerging hot topics did we identify?

KEYWORD INSPIRATION

We can get a more detailed picture of search volume for certain keywords using tools like Google Keyword Planner[39]. This reveals more information about the most common keywords for specific search topics, related phrases, monthly search volume and how much competition they carry. All of this information can help us to work out what the most popular topics are, as well as which terms our competitors are interested in.

As an example, the following screenshot shows results returned for a search on 'virtual reality games':

Figure 13: Google Adwords

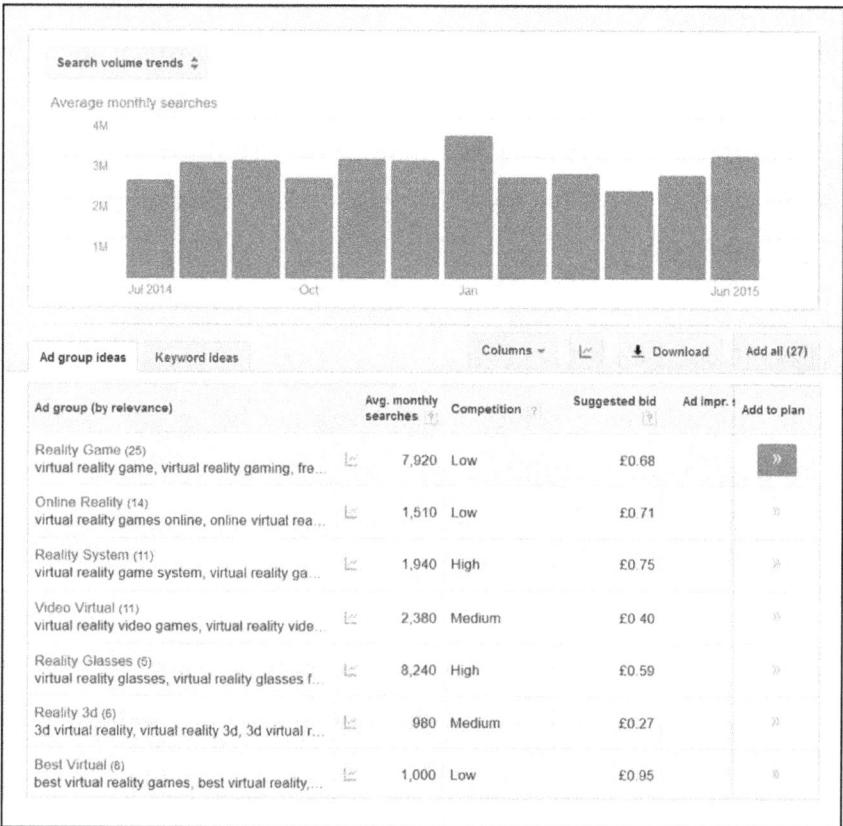

Source: Google AdWords © adwords.google.com

Once we have identified hot keywords, we can use them to inspire content ideas. Identifying the most searched-for terms in a particular field, for a particular demographic, will help us to keep our ideas in the most relevant contexts and maximise our engagement potential.

THE BEATING PULSE

We can keep up to date with what people are talking about right now using websites like Digg[28] and Delicious[25], which identify hot topics in blog posts, articles and videos across the internet.

What content can we create that fits in with the conversations our target audience is having online? Do we have anything useful to bring to the table?

KNOWLEDGE GAPS

There is a difference between customers not being interested in something because they don't care and them not being interested because they don't have enough knowledge or awareness of the topic.

We have an opportunity to grow our market by qualifying future prospects through informative content that highlights and fills certain knowledge gaps. What content can we create to help our audience to better understand these topics and ultimately channel them into our buyer's journey?

What are the most common customer enquiries about our products and services? What are the most prevalent misconceptions in the product area? We can supplement any internal data we can gather by using websites like Quora[80] and Ask MetaFilter[5], which provide huge databases of user-generated questions and answers. This research will also help us to identify the type of language our audience is using to describe their knowledge gaps. Mirroring this language in our content not only creates kinship between our brand and the customer, but also helps to make our content more search friendly.

THINK AMPLIFICATION

When we're thinking about content ideas, let's bear in mind how we might amplify the finished product. In other words, how could we construct or present the content to maximise its reach across social media, search engines and content vending sites?

VIRAL POWER UP

Whether or not something has 'gone viral' depends on the size of the specific target market. For us, we might consider a piece of content aimed at a niche group of 1000 people to have gone viral if 800 of the target group have shared or interacted with it. We should consider the following questions when considering the viral potential of our ideas (we don't need to tick every box, but we should aim for at least one):

1. Is the content something people will want to associate themselves with? People are highly conscious of how they are perceived on social media, so if the content doesn't fit in with what I call the audience's 'virtual identity', it won't get shared widely.

2. Is the content remarkable? Ok, we all come across things that are useful, funny or just interesting, but we don't bang on to

our friends about all of them. The audience will only share content that is remarkable in some way. If our content idea isn't remarkable, we'll struggle to cast it out very far.

3. Will we interest key influencers? As we discussed earlier, key influencers in our field can catapult our content to large portions of our target audiences. If our content idea appeals to the influencers, it has more chance of being well amplified across their networks.

ACTIONABILITY

It is important that we never forget that every piece of content needs to *do* something for us in some way; it has to perform an *action*. For instance, does it drive our audience to the next stage in the journey, encourage them to use another piece of our content or encourage them to sign up to a mailing list?

CROWD SOURCE IDEAS

Whatever their role, every member of staff within our company has a unique perspective on our brand and customers. We can ask them to put forward content ideas that will help, interest or inspire new and existing customers.

When the ideas are in, we can filter them according to their relevance to buyer personas, the buyer's journey and our big aims.

LOOK AT EXISTING CONTENT STOCK

For a moment, imagine you work for a big movie studio and you're looking for the next big blockbuster. Naturally, you review the most successful movies in the studio's portfolio and wonder how you can recreate those magic, super-successful formulas. Finally, you jump out of the canvas chair and squeal: "I've got it! A sequel!"

Of course, sequels, prequels and remakes of successful movies are usually sure fire cash cows for the studios. After all, there is an existing audience base eagerly waiting for more of the story. As content marketers, how can we do the same? Is there any content we can squeeze a little bit more action out of? Can we add anything to existing content to tell more of the story? Can we 'remake' any of our content to make it better?

Now take another look at our content inventory and audit database and concentrate on the most popular pieces of content. Where are the prequel, sequel and remake opportunities?

SIZE MATTERS

According to research by Static Brain[99], only 4% of page views hold users' attention for 10 minutes or more. In response, almost 60% of marketers create new 'snackable' versions of existing assets, according to LookBookHQ[58].

What new content or rehashed existing content can we publish that's quick and easy for our audience to consume?

STEAL INSPIRATION

Although we'll certainly never copy anyone else's work, we should definitely take inspiration from the best content ideas out there. If we find there's a particular piece of content that's being shared, discussed or downloaded widely by our target audience, why not take a closer look at it? Why is it so popular? How could our own version improve this idea?

Coming up with our own unique take on an existing idea isn't as simple as it sounds. We need to make sure our content offers something different, or additional, to the existing content. Duplicating someone else's content is unethical and will do nothing but weaken our message (and our reputation!).

PLATFORMS AND CHANNELS

It's important to frame new content ideas within the channels that our existing customers and prospects are using. There's no point investing time and money to develop content that is not deliverable within the most suitable platforms or channels. What did our research tell us about the platforms and channels that our existing and potential customers are using most?

*   *   *

There are companies out there right now that are stealing your customers' attention. Every second of every day, someone, somewhere is creating content that is designed to distract your audience away from your brand. What are you going to do about it?

There are two options: you can either allow your content competitors to take the lead and simply react to their ideas, or you can take a revolutionary stance and beat a path to your customers' door. I know which you're going to choose.

Armed with everything we have learnt about our customers, we're ideally positioned to seize the best content opportunities by focussing our thoughts in the right areas. Go ahead and start planning your tactics.

REVOLUTIONARY DIRECTIVES

1. Ensure all ideas are inspired by customer needs.
2. Develop ideas around specific stages of the buyer's journey.
3. Keep ideas in the context of the most effective publishing and amplification platform.

17

RESOURCING & PRODUCTION

"Though we may all look at the same things, it does not all follow that we should see them."

John Lubbock

Can you imagine asking a librarian to change the fuel pump on your car? How about asking a nuclear scientist to deliver a baby? Sounds crazy, but it's not a million miles from asking an accountant or a plumber to write a blog or shoot a video.

It's surprising how many companies task untrained and inexperienced staff with copywriting, photography, graphic design and videography projects, but yet still expect top notch results.

Budgetary constraints often mean that professional help is not an option, but there are some things we can do to make best use of the resources we have.

Firstly, we need to consider the main production models, spanning the full range of investment levels. We can then pick and choose the best options for us.

RECRUITING CONTENT PRODUCERS

So, we made the perfect content marketing business case and we have been handed that fabled blank cheque. What do we do now?

Let's hire some dedicated content producers to work within our business. Depending on the types of content we're looking to produce, we'll probably need specialists with copywriting, photography, videography, graphic design and maybe even web development skills.

Having these creative specialists working within our business will help to ensure that they have an integral understanding of our business objectives and are on-hand to seize content opportunities as soon as they arise.

Dedicated creatives will not only produce content to a professional standard, they will also deliver it faster than a moonlighting accountant, plumber or human resources manager.

But how much will dedicated, specialist resources cost? It all depends on the experience of the individual, the specialist sector and the location. The following annual salary ranges may be a useful guide:

- **Copywriter:** $26,000 - $61,000 p/a.
- **Photographer:** $24,437 - $74,744 p/a.
- **Videographer:** $24,000 - $74,000 p/a.
- **Graphic Designer:** $29,500 - $58,000 p/a.

- **Web Developer:** $32,000 - $82,000 p/a.

Data source: PayScale, 2015 www.payscale.com

PER-PROJECT SUPPORT

Ok, so the blank cheque didn't come through, but we have been given a small content marketing budget. How will we make the most of it?

Calling in the professionals to help on special projects will enable us to deliver high-quality content when it matters most.

There are hundreds of companies that offer content production services, along with thousands of freelancers of varying quality. Choosing a local company or freelancer with a good reputation will help keep the costs down, as well as make it more feasible to commission projects at short notice.

Before making any commitments, look at as many examples of the producers' work as possible and take notice of the questions they ask us. In general, if potential content suppliers ask lots of questions about our brand, style, audience and goals, it's a promising sign.

RETAINER AGREEMENTS

Another option is to bring in a specialist content company to support our activities on an on-going basis. My own company, Group Dane, often works with companies in this way. It usually involves a monthly agreement to support the company's strategy, supervision of production activities, performance monitoring and, of course, content creation.

A retainer agreement with a content company can be useful in helping to set up, manage and deliver the strategy, while also getting some expert guidance along the way.

HIDDEN RESOURCES

Now consider that we didn't get any content marketing budget at all. How can we push forward with our plans with existing resources? Although we want to avoid asking staff with no creative skills to produce content, there may be hidden talents within our business. What's the employment history of our staff? Let's dig around and come up with a creative skills matrix to unearth any former journalists, photographers or designers in our midst. We'll also talk to colleagues across the business about our content plans and encourage people with relevant skills to come forward.

HOME-MADE

Useful or interesting content that has been produced by amateurs usually only feels weak if it is pitched as being professional standard. In other words, it feels like a sheep in wolfs' clothing. But truthfully presenting this content as 'home-made' can actually become a selling-point. The real and honest feel of home-made content can create more of a connection with the audience if executed and pitched effectively. But it's important that this approach is only used if it's appropriate to the context. We need to recognise the difference between 'authentic' and 'inappropriate.'

CUSTOMER-GENERATED

Asking customers to create content like reviews and testimonials is a great way of generating highly-influential material. Particularly at the 'Decision' stage of the buyer's journey, our audience will be more influenced by what our customers have to say than anything we do.

Of course, producing this type of content will require organisation, light copyediting and formatting, but can easily be done without too much input from a professional content producer.

Social media is the perfect platform for encouraging customers to submit this type of content, but be careful not to offer incentives for endorsements!

REPURPOSE

Many businesses unwittingly have lots of valuable content lying around that isn't being used effectively. Content like instruction manuals, flow charts, product specifications and model comparisons can be good for repurposing. If the information is somehow interesting or useful to our audience, why not use it?!

* * *

Welcome to your ingenuity test! Please take a seat and make yourself uncomfortable.

I'm now going to hit you with a reality that will probably add a little pressure into the mix, but will ultimately help you to focus your efforts more wisely: **Your success in content marketing**

will not depend on the amount of money spent; in fact, it will hinge on the level of conviction invested.

Many of the companies basking in content marketing glory are running on very limited money and resources. Just look at the father and son who transformed their struggling electronics shop, Magnolia, into an $87M company by publishing a homemade magazine. Or even Foiled Cupcakes who increased revenue goals by 600% by blogging and delivering amazing customer service on social media.

Mix and match production models creatively to suit your financial situation, but remember that the two most important things we can ever invest are *appropriate effort* and *refined judgement.*

If revolution was easy, everyone would be doing it.

REVOLUTIONARY DIRECTIVES

1. Identify the most appropriate production methods to suit your budget, content types and buyer personas.
2. Use budgetary and resourcing limitations to inspire creativity.
3. Recognise the value and influence of customer-generated content.

18

PUBLISHING CHANNELS

"A place for everything and everything in its place."

Benjamin Franklin

Over the past five years, I have been lucky enough to work on a couple of projects with multi-award-winning director and producer, Jon Small.

If you don't recognise his name, you will certainly know of his work. He's directed some of the biggest music videos in history, featuring superstars like Taylor Swift, Billy Joel, Garth Brooks, Whitney Houston, Paul McCartney and Johnny Cash.

In 1986, Jon directed the legendary music video for *Walk This Way*, featuring *Aerosmith* and *Run DMC*, which notably played a major role in the progression of music television.

In the early to mid-eighties, the number of mass media

broadcast channels were limited to say the least. Three main channels ABC, CBS and NBC still dominated network television in the USA and, of course, the World Wide Web wasn't even invented until the tail-end of the decade.

But, broadcast media was changing. By 1985, 68% of all American households (about 60 million) had cable television service, with 88% of those subscribing to a pay cable service like HBO or Showtime.

At this time, MTV (Music Television) was still relatively new, but Jon realised this new platform represented an emerging market. He set up a production company, Picture Vision Pictures, dedicated to developing music television in New York and quickly positioned himself as one of the leading authorities in a developing genre. Fast forward 30 years and a plethora of top awards later, he's still capitalising on technological channel advances in his work today.

Jon's story got me thinking about how we, as content marketers, can capitalise on new platforms and channels, just like Jon did in the eighties. How can we seize opportunities to dominate publishing channels as they emerge? Equally, how can we make the most of existing channels and continually evolve with our audience's needs?

FINDING OUR PLACE

Creating and sourcing fantastic content is hard work, so it is vital that we maximise our return by publishing it where it will get the most exposure.

So far, we have talked extensively about creating content that targets specific personas and stages of the buyer's journey, so it makes little sense to spread it thinly across lots of different channels indiscriminately. We need to be smarter than that.

THE 'SITUATIONAL ANALYSIS'

Before we do anything, we need to have a clear understanding of the current shape we're in. What channels do we have already? What is working and what is not? This will help us to prioritise, budget and plan our next moves.

Joe Pulizzi, founder and CEO of the Content Marketing Institute, calls this stage the "situational analysis".

At this point, all of the information we have accumulated so far, including our buyer personas and buyer's journey, will help to reveal the channels where we can have the most impact with our story. What does our research tell us about the platforms our audience prefers to use?

Joe recommends that we ask ourselves the following three questions:

1. What do we already have that helps us tell this story (e.g. an existing website, blog, Facebook page, Twitter account, corporate materials, article marketing effort, etc.)?
2. What must change in order for us to tell this story (e.g. do we need to add a blog, develop a separate blog, create or revisit our social web strategy)?

3. What must stop (if anything) for us to tell this story (e.g. do we need to stop using Facebook and divert our energy to a blog)?

ALIGNING OBJECTIVES

How do the specific objectives we have attached to each piece of content look against the various channels? Do any particular channels seem to align with, or naturally complement, these objectives?

For example, if one of our goals is to increase brand awareness and the objective for a specific piece of content is to earn 50 social mentions of our brand name, the logical channel might be Twitter.

Some content will fit into more than one channel; if necessary, list primary, secondary and tertiary channels (e.g. primary: YouTube; secondary: brand website; tertiary: Metacafe). Remember, we're only thinking about where the content will physically live, rather than the channels we will use to share or promote it.

DOMINATE, DON'T STAGNATE

We want to dominate conversations and become a big voice in our field, but we can only do this if we have enough impact in the right places. Spreading our efforts thinly across every channel could dilute our rewards.

From a practical point of view, content that is fragmented across many low-use channels is at risk of being forgotten about and stagnating where it sits. This can actually give the impression we have less content available than we do. For example, if we publish one presentation on SlideShare and don't publish again on the channel for 12 months, customers that only touch that channel will think we're inactive.

TO OWN, OR NOT TO OWN

I always feel uneasy when publishing significant volumes of content to third-party-operated platforms. The impending danger is the provider will change publishing rules, limit traffic or visibility of our content, or even introduce (or increase) fees. Wherever there is a toss-up between an owned channel, such as our website or blog, and a rented platform, such as LinkedIn or Facebook, I would personally err towards owned.

PIVOT & STREAMLINE

Whether we're at the start of our content marketing journey, or we are already heavily engaged, it is important that we continually review our use of publishing channels as a matter of course.

The social listening tools we set up earlier as part of our research should be an on-going concern. Where are our customers seeking and accessing content? Think about how our customers' needs are evolving over time and how this ties in with the latest developments in technology and communication trends.

New channels are constantly emerging and often become popular with niche audiences at considerable pace, just as more established channels can wane in popularity overnight.

The market is fluid, so we need to mirror that in our approach to publishing channels. Be ready to kill off failing tactics and seize new opportunities in response to feedback, analytics and evolving behaviours and needs.

*　　　　*　　　　*

Think of your publishing channels as the home of your content. This is where it lives 100% of the time it exists, so you need to make sure it can easily be found and accessed by your target audience at key moments of their journey.

At the end of the day, you're aiming to fundamentally influence the way your target customers think about (and interact with) your brand. If you have any hope of attracting enough attention to drive this change, you need to make sure you're talking to enough of the right people, at the right time, in the *right places*.

Always remember, effective communication lines will form the backbone of your revolution. Choose carefully.

REVOLUTIONARY DIRECTIVES

1. Establish a manageable set of core channels.
2. Strike a healthy balance between content housed on owned channels and "rented" ones (Facebook, Twitter, etc.).
3. Be ready to add or drop channels according to customer behaviour.

19

CONTENT AMPLIFICATION

"Things do not happen.

Things are made to happen."

John F. Kennedy

Say the words 'Scouse Bird' to anyone in Liverpool and they will know exactly what you're talking about. In fact, they'll probably also have a Marmite-style love/hate opinion on the subject. But, chances are you are not from Liverpool, so let me explain.

Scouse Bird, is a writer and media personality with a difference. The creation of writer and businesswoman, Steph Johnson, Scouse Bird is a fictional character that plays on a number of regional stereotypes, with lashings of fun and irony. Scouse Bird writes articles about everything her target audience is interested in, from fashion and beauty, to travelling and dating.

Sounds like a lot of fun, but Scouse Bird is big business for Steph, who has built up an empire on the back of her Facebook and Twitter presence. With an average of 200k visits to her website every month, more than 70% of the site's traffic comes from earned social media referrals (including almost 100k from Facebook and 50k from Twitter). The fan base is loyal but growing steadily, with 62% returning visitors.

My company, Group Dane, started working with Steph/Scouse Bird back in in 2013. We were called in to develop a new website to form the hub of the brand's owned media content, Scouse Bird Problems. The site is where the bulk of the money is made, through sponsored articles, product reviews, endorsements and in-page advertising. In case you're wondering how much Steph spends on advertising and promotion to drive this volume of traffic, the answer is: zero. So what's her secret?

For starters, everything Scouse Bird publishes hits that magical sweet spot we talked about earlier. Her specialist knowledge and the audience's interests come together in perfect harmony. Add to this the fact that Scouse Bird packs her posts with the content her audience either want to be associated with, or want to share for comedic or empathetic value, and you quickly see how the brand has become a viral powerhouse.

Scouse Bird bolsters her ever-growing influence by frequently publishing guest blogs alongside her own posts, while also syndicating her content across the sites of other key influencers in the field.

Although Scouse Bird is followed by people all over the world, the bulk of her support comes from masses of loyal fans largely concentrated around the Liverpool city region. This means that companies operating in this area (from small chains to multi-nationals) are falling over themselves to be talked about by Scouse Bird. And when you look at the audience engagement figures and level of influence the brand has, it's not difficult to see why.

Although Scouse Bird Problems is a media publishing company rather than a content marketing initiative, we can learn a lot from Steph's amplification techniques. Let's take a closer look at how we can replicate some of her tactics, in conjunction with a few other approaches.

So far I've mentioned the term 'amplification' a few times throughout the book, without any real definition. To explain: 'content amplification' is about increasing the reach of our content by employing marketing tactics. In a nutshell, it's about marketing our content marketing. It sounds like an odd concept, but bear with me...

TIME FOR OUR PAY-OFF

We have invested a lot of time so far in researching, planning and producing content, so now we need to maximise our return by getting it out there to as much of our target audience as possible. Our aim is to magnify its profile so it can rise above everything else out there that is distracting our audience.

Some of our amplification options are relatively low effort and low cost, while others require more work and, in some cases, financial outlay. We'll look more closely at some of our options in just a minute.

AN OBJECTIVE STEER

As we've repeatedly discussed so far, every single piece of content we create has its own specific objectives. We need to consider what we want to achieve with each piece. Are we aiming to drive more traffic back to the website? Do we want to boost brand exposure? Is the aim to grow authority in a specific area?

Before we start to turn up the volume of our voice, it's important that we take the time to estimate just how much exposure the content is likely to need in order to fulfil its purpose. Look at the metrics we attached to our objectives for each piece. With this in mind, we can think about what platforms and amplification methods will be most appropriate.

AMPLIFICATION TYPES

There are three main types of platform for amplification: 'owned media', 'paid media' and 'earned media', with a fusion in the middle, known as 'converged media'.

Figure 14: Converging amplification methods

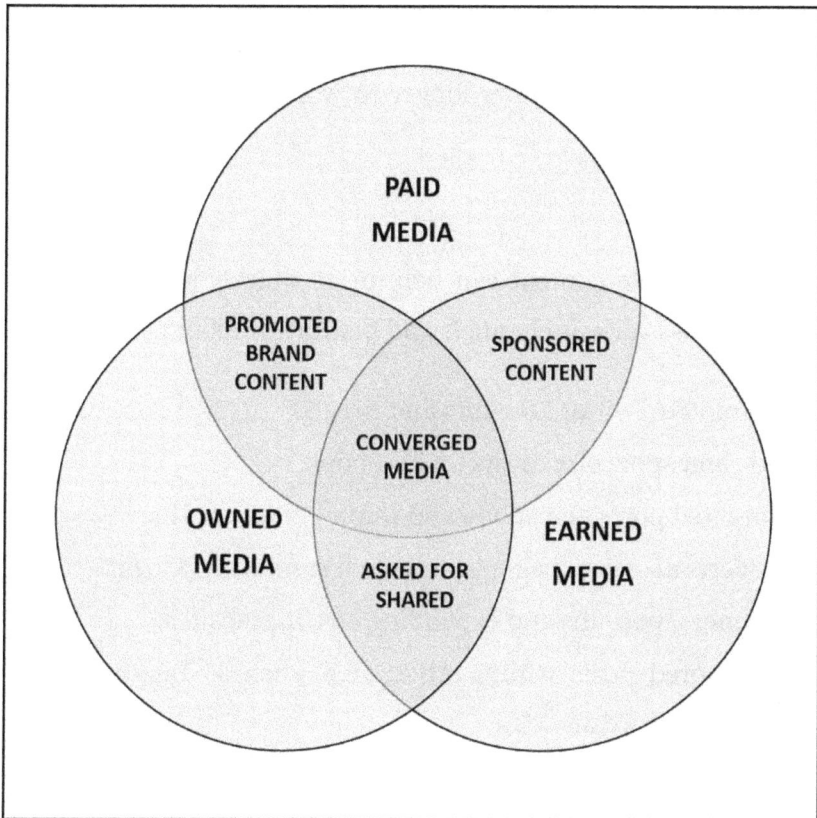

1. OWNED MEDIA

The content that our brand has complete control over is known as owned media. Examples include platforms we own, such as:

- Blog sites, websites and microsites.
- Social profiles, such as Twitter, Facebook, LinkedIn and Google Plus.
- Email distribution lists.

The main benefit of owned media is that we can publish and promote anything we want, in any format, often at very little cost. The downside for most businesses is that it's more difficult to get attention and it usually takes longer to work than paid or earned media.

2. PAID MEDIA

Paying to promote content can help us to quickly generate more exposure across various channels and platforms. Examples include:

- Promoted Twitter accounts and tweets.
- Ads and sponsored posts on Facebook.
- Targeted posts and sponsored InMail on LinkedIn.
- Adverts above and alongside search results on Google.
- Banners, pop-ups and expanding ads on websites.
- Sponsored posts within other sites, such as BuzzFeed and Huffington Post.
- Sponsored and display advertising on YouTube.
- Embedded content or banners within apps.

The main benefits of promoting content on paid channels are much greater reach and faster rates of content propagation. On the flipside, paid media will be seen as advertising (and often dismissed) by our audience if it isn't pitched and targeted perfectly.

3. EARNED MEDIA

This is content that is spread by third parties through activities like PR and word of mouth. Earned media has 'viral' tendencies which often proliferate through social mentions, shares, reposts, reviews and recommendations. Examples include:

- Social sharing.
- Guest blogging.
- References and links from bloggers.
- Mentions and retweets by influencers.
- Press coverage.

The great thing about earned media is that it means others are actively promoting or engaging with our content. Remember that neutral, third-party voices create authentic social proof for our brand. The difficulty with earned media is the fact that we can't buy or create it; rather we have to optimise our content for engagement and sharing.

4. CONVERGED MEDIA

Converged media mixes owned, earned or paid platforms. This convergence between media types is the amplification sweet spot. This is where we are able to get the best of all three platform types by setting them to work together seamlessly.

By aiming for a converged media approach to amplification, we can dramatically reduce our financial investment. We can get our amplification strategy off to a start by using owned media to generate earned media.

It is smart to start new content campaigns with owned media and then gauge the effectiveness of the content. We can then decide whether or not to implement paid media tactics to further accelerate amplification.

OPTIMISING FOR EARNED

Whenever we are creating content, we should be thinking about how we can optimise it for earned media. How we can make the content as attractive to our audience as possible, while also maximising its shareability? Think about Scouse Bird's success with earned media and its roots in a heightened awareness of the target audience's needs.

This is where we need to put our journalist's hat on.

Use the most attractive and highly-relevant titles, images and propositions that will entice our target customers. But, we must not use gutter press tactics; keep our brand values at the heart of everything we do and remember that no amount of attention is worth eroding our reputation. Always avoid tricking our audience with 'click baiting' tactics, such as misleading headlines or empty promises.

When promoting the content, we also need to sow some seeds to encourage advocates and influencers to interact with our content and share it with their own audience. We can start by making sure they are aware of the content. For example, could we target a specific piece of content towards a key influencer on Twitter, using mentions and relevant hashtags?

BUYER'S JOURNEY STAGES

Think about the buyer's journey we mapped out earlier. What do our buyer personas and market research tell us about where our audience is at each stage of the journey? What media channels are they using to look for solutions to their problems?

Our amplification tactics should support all of these stages, from Awareness and Discovery through to the Consideration, Purchase and Advocate and Reconvert stages.

TOOLS

There are a number of tools that can help us to manage our content amplification activities and also make it easier for our customers to share our content. Tools to consider include:

- AddThis[2] allows us to implement simple ways for visitors to share content from our owned channels, such as share buttons that allow content to be distributed across multiple platforms and social networks, driving traffic back to our website.

- Outbrain[71] is a content discovery platform that helps to promote articles, videos, slideshows, infographics, and even earned media across high-traffic, well-known media properties, such as CNN, Slate and ESPN.

- Zemanta[120] compiles original content and then optimises it for multiple distribution hubs, such as promoted recommendations, in-stream advertisements, in-text ads, and sponsored content on top media sites.

- Cision[14] provides tools to create, publish, drive, and analyse branded content. By targeting engaged audiences on top-tier websites, it aims to increase brand exposure and drive traffic.

*　　　*　　　*

Ultimately, content amplification is about connecting dots. It's about linking our content to our target audience, in the right places, at optimal moments.

Of course, the more we understand our audience and their journey, the better informed our amplification tactics will be. Let all of the insights you have gathered so far give you the confidence to experiment with techniques and adapt your approach as you go. Remember, content rarely achieves massive reach just by chance; it's usually the result of a heightened understanding of the audience and a series of educated risks.

Be bold, have courage and never rely on blind hope!

REVOLUTIONARY DIRECTIVES

1. Combine owned, paid and earned methods for best results.
2. Use tools and dashboards to help manage amplification activities on-the-fly.
3. Align amplification efforts with where our personas are in the buyer's journey.

-STEP FIVE-

HOLDING POWER

20

MEASURING & MONITORING

"In business, words are words; explanations are explanations, promises are promises, but only performance is reality."

Harold Geneen

A few years ago, I did some acting. I started off with stage plays, before going on to do quite a lot of short films, web series and a couple of b-movie features. Wow, I had made it!

In some ways, being involved with film productions felt more glamorous than theatre. This was partly because of screening events in swish venues (basically parties), those glossy publicity photographs and, of course, the strangely satisfying IMDb records, preserved online for all eternity. I was young and I felt like a movie star! Yet, I desperately missed something about performing on stage.

The intimacy and the immediate audience connection just isn't there when you're performing for the camera. After all, it can be months, even years, between the Director shouting "it's a wrap" and the audience seeing the final edit. As a theatre actor, on the other hand, I had the audience right there with me. My eyes and ears were like real-time monitoring devices that enabled me to test and validate my performance on-the-fly. Moment by moment, I could adjust and adapt according to silences, laughter, tension and applause.

As a content marketer, I still feel like I need that instant audience validation. I'm always looking for their approval and seeking the rewarding feeling that comes with knowing my efforts are valued. The only way we're ever going to succeed with content marketing is if we're obsessed with wooing our target audience. Indeed, it's the pursuit of that satisfying feeling that makes me successful in my efforts. And let's face it, what are our customers going to do with their approval? They're going to pay it back in loyalty, advocacy and years of repeat business. Get obsessed with giving the audience what they want!

I've found that content marketing is not a million miles from theatre acting in the way we can monitor and adapt to our audience as we go, using real-time analytics and social interactions as our eyes and ears. Are they enthralled or bored, cheering or booing? We can use this instant feedback to continually adapt our performance, make sure we're holding attention and confirm in our own minds that we're giving the audience everything they need from our story.

When we were talking about setting goals earlier, I stressed that every single one needs to be measurable. Furthermore, our metrics have to specifically tell us something about the value of every single one of our activities.

Across all industries, there is a real problem with the measurement of content marketing activity. Just 8% of businesses consider themselves to be 'very successful' at tracking content marketing return on investment, according LinkedIn Technology Marketing Community[57].

Most businesses fall down by looking too broadly at general numbers like page views and shares, without interpreting this data into actionable insights. In fact, according to research by Contently[21], 90% of marketers don't feel that their key content metrics effectively measure business results.

Why not take this as an opportunity to get ahead of our competitors?! What do we need to look for and how can we translate our findings into actions that will help tip the scales?

BACK TO THE BIG AIM

The only way to accurately measure our success is to constantly relate the metrics we gather to our big aims, goals and objectives. Rather than just reporting raw figures like website visits, video views, and social interactions, we need to create a narrative interpretation of our performance. For example, how do social interactions contribute to the bigger picture? Are they leading to customer enquiries or helping to amplify content to bigger audiences? What do spikes in customer activity tell us about the resonance of a certain topic? These questions will help us to work out the things we're doing well and the things we need to change.

CAPTURING LEADS

So far, we have talked about improving our brand image, getting on our audience's radar and building confidence in our product. But what is it all for ultimately? We want to convert our content users into customers, so we have to look specifically at how much impact we're having on lead generation.

Of course, it's difficult to directly attribute our content marketing activity to sales figures, as, by definition, it doesn't usually direct customers to the buy button. However, we can (and should) be tracking the leads that our activity is generating.

We will now take a closer look at the impact our content marketing activity is having on lead generation:

- **Email subscriptions:** Along with measuring the number of subscriptions to newsletters, we can feed names and other details we capture directly into our email marketing system, for example MailChimp[59] or Pure 360[78]. This information goes some of the way towards indicating how our subscribers relate to the buyer personas we were targeting. Did we attract the types of customers we set out to?

- **Downloads:** Quite easily, we can track the number of 'open downloads' (where a customer doesn't have to enter any details to access the content) by setting up 'Events' in Google

Analytics. For 'gated downloads' (where the customer has to enter some details before they can access the content), we can, again, feed the information we capture into our email marketing system or our CRM (client relationship management system), such as Salesforce[85] or Zoho[121]. This enables us to track the progress of our relationship with the lead following this interaction with our content.

- **Enquiries and call backs:** By adding Google Analytics 'Events' code to specific links, we can pin down the specific piece of content a prospect was referred by. To track telephone enquiries, we can either set up specific telephone numbers to channel enquiries that originate from content, or build in questions to the telephone operators' script.

- **Referrals:** By using features that allow our audience to refer (or send) content to friends or colleagues, we can capture lead data from both the sender and receiver, also feeding this directly into our CRM.

MARKET AUTOMATION

While analytics platforms like Google Analytics[37] and Web Trends[115] can provide numbers and highlight behavioural patterns, this information is not tied to specific individuals. We can dig a lot deeper using market automation systems like Marketo[61], Hubspot[45] and Eloqua[29].

These systems harvest reliable lead data by tracking specific individuals as they travel through the buyer's journey, even scoring how 'hot' each lead is by interpreting their behavioural characteristics.

Market automation systems don't come cheap, with annual subscriptions typically between $10,000 and $50,000, but if budget allows, they offer highly detailed reporting capabilities.

BRAND PERCEPTIONS

The best way to measure how perceptions of our brand are changing is by looking at the sentiments of interactions across social media. Are we increasing favourable mentions and reducing negative ones?

We can conduct a study into awareness of our brand and products as a result of our content marketing activity. There are a number of standalone tools that can help us with sentiment analysis (also known as opinion mining), including some built into social platforms (such as Facebook). These tools analyse qualitative metrics, based around the use of words in relation to attitudes, emotions and opinions. Look at Radian6[81], Social Mention[96] and free custom dashboards in Netvibes[69].

TRAFFIC

While traffic doesn't always equate to sales, it does tell us whether our content activities are generating interest in our products and services. We can use Google Analytics to look at the volume of traffic visiting our websites, along with measuring product-related touch-points, such as app usage and any customer enquiry data we can gather.

By looking specifically at where traffic is coming from, we can work out exactly what content is having the most leverage across the buyer's journey.

Are there any signs that we are creating a buzz around our brand? Is our content strengthening the link between our company and our product area? To help us answer these questions, we can look for increases in searches for the types of products we offer that include our brand name.

TIME IS OF THE ESSENCE

One way to measure how engaged our audience is with specific pieces of content is by looking at how much time they spend on it. Look at things like time-on-page data from Google Analytics and video view durations in YouTube. Surprisingly, less than half of all marketers measure this kind of data, according to research by Contently[21].

SOCIAL TRACTION

The majority of marketers (68%) measure their social media activities, according to Social Media Examiner[95].

By measuring the social interactions each piece of content generates, we can better understand how deeply it is resonating with the target audience. How many tweets, retweets, likes, shares, comments and mentions is each piece earning? What are the channels and amplification platforms that are showing the most activity?

Here, we're interested in spikes in activity across all social platforms. What are we doing specifically that is generating this interest and what are we getting out of it? For example, are these spikes either leading web traffic to other content in our portfolio or generating email subscribers, customer enquiries or even purchases? Understanding this will help us to focus our efforts on the activities that generate those 'hot actions' among our target audience.

DOWN TO BRASS TACKS

How much is all of this engagement worth versus the time and money we have invested? We can use all of the lead data we have gathered to report the sales-lift among customers that have been exposed to our content marketing activity.

Whether we're spending money on content generation or using company hours, we need to report just how much we're spending versus the amount of engagement we're generating in return.

REPORTING

Although we'll measure and monitor each piece of content continuously, we'll need to report more broadly on our activities at certain points. When we made the business case earlier, we alluded to what we would achieve. Are we getting there?

The main purpose of the report is to demonstrate the impact we're having on the business as a whole. We'll do this by pulling together all of the data we have gathered and create a narrative that interprets the results. Remember to put all of our metrics in the context of specific big aims, goals and objectives.

*　　　*　　　*

At the end of the day, you need to be able to answer one question: did it work?

I can't stress enough how important it is to focus only on metrics that directly relate to our big aim, goals and objectives. Don't waste time collecting data and reporting on anything else. In my experience, information that doesn't prove or justify our activity will just distract us from those actionable nuggets of insight, not to mention bloat our reports and encourage extraneous questions from above that are impossible to answer.

In a nutshell, by focussing on the right things, we'll keep our wits sharp and allow us to cut loose ineffective efforts that are slowing us down.

The concept is simple: collect the right information, make informed judgements and change things that aren't working. Our mantra goes like this: 'GAUGE - ACT – MEASURE – ADAPT'.

REVOLUTIONARY DIRECTIVES

1. Only measure things that are important.
2. Tie all objectives to measurable outcomes.
3. Measure and adapt content continually.

21

A LEADER EMERGES

"If you want to change the world,

pick up your pen and write."

Martin Luther King, Jr

As I write the concluding words of this book, I am 36,000 feet above the Atlantic Ocean, somewhere between London and New York City. In the three hours since this 450 ton machine lifted off, I have been thinking about the founding fathers of aviation, Alcock and Brown, Louis Blériot, and, of course, the Wright brothers.

I can only imagine the scale of the challenges, dangers and cynicism these pioneers faced throughout their endeavours. Yet, they persevered.

Whether you're just starting out with content marketing, or looking to bolster existing efforts, take inspiration from the big revolutionary thinkers that precede you. At times you too will face challenge, doubt and opposition, but you must be headstrong, confident and assured in your thinking.

Throughout the book, we've covered each of the key steps towards content marketing revolution, but we haven't talked about one crucial factor that will ultimately determine success: *YOU*. I'm going to leave you with three characteristics you'll need to embrace before you can lead your charge.

DEDICATION

Every revolutionary leader has one thing in common: an unwavering dedication to the cause. Adopting a dogged spirit will help you to overcome challenges and adapt to setbacks in order to drive the outcomes you want. The more dedicated you are to your objectives, the better your returns will be.

AUDACITY

By definition, revolution can only be achieved with change, so don't allow your decisions to be guided by the status quo. Your revolution will be driven by the risks and opportunities you choose to seize, so arm yourself with the research intelligence you'll need to confidently make bold decisions. With no risk, there is no revolution.

FOCUS

With sharp focus on your objectives, you'll make more of the right decisions and keep your strategy on the right track. Align all of your thinking with your overarching big aim and let it be your compass.

*   *   *

Every market, in every sector, across the globe is affected by the cultural shift towards greater autonomy in buying decisions. With customers putting more emphasis than ever on their relationship with the seller, content marketing is not as much a choice as it is a prerequisite for today's brands.

Right now, you have an opportunity to satisfy your customers' needs and enrich customer touch points with valuable, brand-defining content. The revolution is already underway – it is up to you to decide who is going to lead it.

Get out there and shake up your customers' worlds with valuable engagements, redefine your brand and seize your rightful place at the top of your market.

So what are you waiting for?

REVOLUTIONARY THINKERS

"I am not afraid of storms for I am learning

how to sail my ship."

Louisa May Alcott

Throughout my career, I have been fortunate enough to work with some of today's most accomplished content professionals, who are each making waves at the top of their industries.

In my experience, the most successful content marketers watch, listen and learn from their peers. They take every opportunity to absorb valuable insight from the leading lights, both within their fields and beyond. For me, the most fascinating people are those that are consistently creating impact with audiences using a mixture of best practice and their own home-grown methodologies.

The following pages are filled with contributions from some of the finest content professionals, as they explain how they go about devising, pitching and creating compelling content.

STORYTELLING: MARK DAVIES MARKHAM

Mark Davies Markham is an award winning writer for Theatre, Radio and Television. He has written for some of the most iconic television series in the UK, including *EastEnders, Band of Gold* and *This Life*, while his theatre credits include the hit UK West End Musical *Taboo* (Music by Boy George), which was winner of two Olivier Awards.

INGREDIENTS FOR A GREAT STORY

There are a few elements that you'll find in all of your favourite stories. Let's start with 'attention'. If you don't have the audiences' attention straight away, you probably won't have an audience for very long. Think about how you can capture their interest and how you will provide value in the first few seconds. Whatever you do to capture attention early on, keep it highly relevant and faithful to the rest of the content.

The next ingredient to think about is 'crisis'. From Shakespeare to soap operas, the best stories are built around a problem that needs to be solved. Think about it, an antagonist would be pretty redundant if they didn't bring with them an imminent crisis. Ask yourself what predicament forms the foundation of your narrative and make this clear. What problem does your content solve (whether that is in the world of the story or within the world of your audience)?

One of the themes that cuts through most stories is one of 'change'. After all, it represents a journey of some kind. It could be change for the better or worse, a new angle on an old problem, or even a journey towards greater wisdom. But of course, you don't always have to follow the anticipated or desired journey. The road to Damascus may be clear, but will you follow it?

Of course, resolution is the part of the story that the audience craves the most. You don't have to provide a complete resolution, but you and the audience always need to be aware of what it might be. What is the resolving act? Will you deliver it or not? Either way, be clear on what it is.

At the end of the story, the audience has to feel like it was worthwhile. There needs to be a sense of catharsis: "I want to carry on living."

KEEPING THE AUDIENCE ENGAGED

It's no secret that the best stories have great hooks that leave the audience wanting to find out what happens next. Those hooks can be built around intrigue, jeopardy, suspense, fascination, empathy, compassion or necessity. But, in every case, these hooks have to relate back to either the characters/individuals we're portraying or the audience themselves. Whether it's a fictional story or a real-life scenario, if the people that live inside of your narrative resonate with the audience, our audience will be much more engaged.

It's important to remember that the audience doesn't always want to be *told*, so don't extradite them by giving away too much upfront. In fact, why not encourage them to do some of the work themselves? Give them something to think about, work out or even discuss after they have consumed your content. Do this well and your audience will feel much more invested.

The key thing to remember is that we don't ever want our audience to be ahead of us. If they can predict the next part of the story, we're either writing cliché or telling them something they already know. If you're retelling a familiar story or reasserting something they already know, put an original spin on it. If you don't make your own mark, the audience won't remember you.

KEEP THE AUDIENCE COMING BACK

The secret to keeping the audience coming back is to really know them inside out. What do they want and need? What causes them joy and grief? What sort of battles do they face? The more you know about your audience, the more effectively you can use your content to fulfil their needs. Whether you are solving problems, entertaining or imparting wisdom, give the audience what they want and they will be back for more.

Again, characters are also important here. If your audience identifies with your characters, they are more likely to want to follow their journeys and find out what happens to them. Who are your own favourite characters and why do you chose to follow them?

A CREATIVE STATE OF MIND

As a writer, I always try to be open to new ideas and free thinking. This means being acutely aware of my surroundings and things that are happening that most people wouldn't notice. Keeping your eyes (and mind) open is a great way to notice interesting things and form original ideas. It's crucial to develop good listening skills. Listen to people, your audience, your friends, your enemies, even your competitors. A good idea is only good if it is relevant in its context. How can you ever be open to relevant ideas if you aren't aware of the world around you and what matters to the people in it?

For me, creativity comes and goes. Sometimes, I find that ideas flow and other times they don't come as easily. The key is to capitalise on the good ideas when you have them. I usually think carefully about all of my ideas before I decide to invest more time in them. I try to dissect the idea, think about its potential, consider how much room it has to grow and, crucially, how relevant it is to the intended audiences' needs.

The key is to run with the creativity when it comes and not to force it too much when it doesn't. There are things that some writers do to help encourage a more creative state of mind, such as listening to certain types of music, going for a walk in the park, taking a hot bath, etc. Every writer is different, so you need to work out what works best for you and run with it.

*   *   *

VIDEO: ALEXANDER BIRRELL

Alexander Birrell is an international filmmaker, having written and directed productions in the UK, USA and Italy. He is an expert in all areas of cinematography and visual storytelling, with a pedigree that includes a mentorship from director of *In Bruges*, *Seven Psychopaths* and *Six Shooter*, Martin McDonagh, and an MA in Filmmaking from the London Film School.

AVOIDING COMMON MISTAKES

The most common mistake made by non-professionals making videos is the belief that the actual shooting is less important than how it will eventually be put together in the editing.

There is often a lack of decision and competency in the selection or creation of shots, framing and lighting and the resulting footage can be very difficult to put together in a meaningful way. This problem comes about due to a lack of a chance to become familiar with cameras, lenses and lighting equipment. A lot of people have access to a digital editing system and can easily teach themselves to fairly advanced levels with enough practice. As the actual shooting equipment tends to be expensive to buy or hire, there is little opportunity for non-professionals to familiarise themselves with it. I would say that the most important thing to remember is that if you don't get it on set, you don't have it. Frequent technical mistakes include either inadequate lighting or believing that no lighting is necessary, reliance on autofocus which should always be disabled, poor audio quality or a mistaken belief that the on camera microphone will be enough (it almost never is). Not using a tripod and constant use of a zoom are also common indicators of lack of experience.

BEST QUALITY FOR A LIMITED BUDGET

Thorough pre-planning is the best way to deal with a limited budget. If you can have an idea of every shot you need in advance you can make an accurate list of every piece of equipment, location, crewmember and 'actor' that you would need at any given moment. Even given the best circumstances, it is unlikely that you would get all the shots you think you need but at least you have a working document to adapt as the days progress.

It's also important to tailor your video to the budget as much as possible. There are a million ways to impart any message or tell any story and you should look for the most expressive way possible within your means. The best place to put the money really depends on the project but it is important to always allow enough funds for transport and catering if you employing people to make your video as an army really does march on its stomach.

ADVANTAGES OF VIDEO

Video connects more directly with an audience because it engages all of the audience's senses at once. We watch, listen and read at the same time. Video also has the ability to directly relay information to us in an entertaining way. There are also a number of ways in which video can be used to demonstrate something exactly how it is. For example, a technical demonstration is very dry and confusing if shown by text and can suffer from flawed or subjective descriptions of objects or processes. In a video you can actually show how something should be done in a clear and objective way.

ENTICING THE PLAY BUTTON

The title of a video along with the still frame image you select for the thumbnail are the most important things in getting someone to watch your video. It is often even worth creating a special image for the thumbnail. If you are trying to demonstrate something then clearly state it in the title or else pose a question, be ironic or even make a pun on the name. All these things attract interest. Then the most important thing is that the first few seconds of the video are interesting and engaging. It's so easy now to click off something if it doesn't grab you immediately so that's the challenge. Endless graphics and titles at the opening are not a good idea, get right to the point.

D.I.Y. VERSUS PROFESSIONAL HELP

It really depends on you and your needs whether you produce the video yourself or go to a professional. If you have the technical skills and the ideas then go for it but you won't save any time or money by thinking that a quick Handycam film will replace a carefully put together professional film. It is definitely the time to call a professional if your video will involve complicated equipment, professional performers or if you are aiming for any kind of advanced graphics or shots. Even if you are only interviewing people you work with, you might get better results having them interviewed by professionals that they don't know and will take more seriously.

EDITORIAL CONSIDERATIONS

The single most important factor for a successful edit is to know what you are going for in advance and shoot towards getting that. This will mean that the resulting footage will be a lot easier to put together. You need to make sure you get multiple takes of everything you need, both audio and video. Aim to shoot more than you need, but never less. If you are doing interviews then don't just film the answers but also the questions and pauses, you don't know when you might need them. Also, avoid holes in the audio by recording a room tone or atmosphere track of every location you shoot in.

ENGAGING THE AUDIENCE

The best way for businesses to engage audiences is to borrow the techniques of narrative cinema. Any video can be made more dynamic by the structured editing of well-shot and framed material. Create interesting images, move the camera and pick attractive locations and the production value of the video will shoot right up. Music and graphics are also very important. They can date very quickly and even feel patronising if they try to be too on trend so it pays to be careful.

CREATING COMPELLING VIDEO

The thing to keep in mind all the time is the objective of the video and what you want the audience to go away with. This makes it a lot easier to find the right approach in terms of shooting style and tone. If you can find a 'hook' to build your video around, create some kind of story or aim that reaches a conclusion. You'll find this is much more compelling than simply giving information.

INFLUENCING THE AUDIENCE

If you're hoping to influence an audience in some way then it is best to directly state your point and then present compelling evidence. An example would be to do a kind of three-act structure video. Present a common problem, show how your product or service is the best way to deal with it and then illustrate all the reasons why, ending with a demonstration. You could also reverse this by directly showing your product or service in the beginning and then developing a narrative that shows how vital it is and how difficult it would be to do without it. Audiences are very good at sensing insincerity and overselling, so the best results come from not overdramatizing and being clear, honest and direct.

*   *   *

NEWS FEATURES: DEBORA FOUGERE

Debora Fougere is an award-winning journalist and television producer, with a top-flight background in news, PR and fashion marketing. Her career has involved producing news for shows like ABC's *Good Morning America* and CNN's *Anderson Cooper 360*. She travelled extensively throughout the USA and Europe, researching, writing and conducting interviews with leading global figures. Debora has received Emmy, Peabody and DuPont/Columbia Journalism awards for her contributions to coverage of the September 11th attacks, the Indonesian Tsunami and Hurricane Katrina.

PITCHING THE AUDIENCE

I have never been a big believer in the 'lowest common denominator' theory in selling stories to an audience, though, in newsrooms everywhere I would admit to being in the minority in that belief. Cutting stories from a newscast, say, or a website in America because they take place overseas and no one here would be interested is an idea that is both antiquated and disrespectful. Yes, sometimes it's the job of the media simply to report on news that is happening now in our own backyard, but there are times when it's our job to teach that audience about something happening, maybe thousands of miles away, letting them know this is something they must know about, a story that must be told.

Selling stories you know will interest your audience, or 'news you can use', is easy: short, sharp headlines, quick teasers that make them stand up and take notice, like "will you need your umbrella tomorrow?", "how much will you pay for milk next week", or the always popular scare-em headlines like "is your fridge killing you?" have a built-in interest. Teachable stories are far more difficult to sell. That's when the need for the perfect picture and the right words are essential; "we'll take you to a place where 10,000 children are dying every wee", or, "here's a story you need to hear", words that play on the emotions of the audience are a good way to pique their interest.

HOLDING INTEREST

Having a great story to tell, a story you believe in, is the best way to keep an audience interested. Good, solid writing is the foundation for any piece, be it online, in print or using video, writing in a way that keeps revealing more and more as the story goes on, like peeling back the layers of an onion. We've all read or heard stories that say everything in the first few paragraphs, then limp to a conclusion. Think about the stories you've read or watched and closed the magazine, switched the channels or clicked off halfway through because you began to feel you were hearing the same thing over and over again. The goal is to keep hitting them with another piece of information, another wow moment, all the way through. One very important rule: always deliver on what you promised at the start. A sexy headline followed by a story that doesn't answer the questions or address the issues stated will only anger your audience, and once that trust is broken, they won't come back. It's called 'anticappointment', and it has the same effect in an over-hyped product as it does in a news story that doesn't deliver.

STRUCTURE

To use, or not to use, the news pyramid depends on the kind of piece you're writing or producing. If it's a hard news piece, you really have no choice but to begin with the newest information, move on to a little background, or 'nut graph', then finish off with whatever additional information is available, like historical facts or reaction. It's not my favourite way to write, but it is simple, you have no choice but to structure a breaking or developing news story that way. Given the choice, I would rather write pieces that have more of an emotional impact. Here's an example: I recently worked on a piece about New York's rent regulations, which were about to expire. It could have been as dry as dust, filled with numbers and percentages. Instead, I started with a quote from a woman, an immigrant grandmother at risk of losing her flat should the regulations end. Her story ran through the piece, giving an otherwise dull story a human face. Beginning a story with the most emotional or shocking or provocative quote or sound bite is a great way to grab the audience. It gives you more freedom, as well, to allow the story to flow naturally, to introduce the history, background, facts and figures organically, giving the audience a story to buy into.

THE RIGHT MIX OF MEDIA

If there is one old adage that is absolutely true, it is "a picture is worth a thousand words", and a great picture is worth many more than that. If you have fantastic images, whether still or video, that's what should take precedence in a piece, with text used only as a bridge, or for explanation, when needed. I believe that should be your first consideration: does the text take a back seat to spectacular images, or do the images simply bolster the piece? If the images are there to support the words, then they need to do that literally. You can't leave it to your viewer or reader to try to figure out what you were trying to convey, it's just too much work. Images also shouldn't be extraneous, they have to make sense. If you're lucky, you'll have something that's creatively and beautifully shot, but if you're talking about a giant red dog, you should see a giant red dog. It's the images that will evoke emotion, before the words.

EDITORIAL STYLE

Research, research, research. One of the most important, and sometimes most difficult, things about writing and producing for news is capturing the voice of the person who will voice over the script. You have to listen, again and again, to his or her reads of different types of stories. The cadence, the inflections, the wording, the words that give them problems. Failing to capture the voice of the speaker is the quickest way to lose that job. The same is true for the publication or website you're writing for. If you don't know what they cover, how they cover it, and the voice they convey, you won't write for them for long. There are things I know about my own writing style: I'd prefer to write with a kind of snarky humour, and I love alliteration. If the people publishing the piece don't share that love, it has to go. However, as a writer, I recognise the almost insane attachments we have for our words and our style, and how ferociously we'll fight to make the rest of the world understand that our words, our style, are right. Just ask any copy editor. Resisting the urge to educate them is the best way to keep writing.

SERIES AND THEMES

Sometimes, the links are obvious. Other times, not so much. Right from the pitch stage you should make sure there's something, even the smallest thread that makes each piece fit. Think of it as matching a shirt to a tie. The patterns may be off, but if there's one little pop of colour in each that matches, you can make it work. If, however, you feel like you're really straining, if it screams, "which of these things is not like the others?", you need to let it go. One thing you have to remember: your readers don't know what you know. They probably don't work in news or for a website. They don't know what goes on in your decision-making process as you're putting together theme pieces, and they don't care. They are looking for good content, interesting stories, something they didn't know. If you're trying to fit a piece into a bigger theme, all you really need to ask is, is this answering a question that hasn't been answered yet in the other stories? Over-thinking can become your worst enemy. If you keep digging deeper, finding out more, discovering other ways to surprise your readers or viewers, they will read another story, they will search for more. If you can do that, you've done your job, as far as they're concerned.

*   *   *

PR: SAMANTHA MARTIN

Samantha Martin is Media Relations Manager at the University of Liverpool, which is part of the prestigious Russell Group of universities. Throughout her 11 years' experience in PR, Samantha has been responsible for promoting high-profile research, including the University's contribution to the discovery of the Higgs Boson in 2012. She has worked across a range of channels, including digital, print, television and radio, collaborating with some of the biggest media organisations in the UK, including BBC, ITV, The Guardian and The Times.

IDEA DEVELOPMENT

Developing content for a news site at a higher education institution starts by carefully considering the needs of the organisation, its audience, long-term goals, and how it wants to present itself to a global market in an increasingly competitive environment.

News production in higher education is influenced by funding streams, government agendas, media headlines and reaching people in areas where research will make the biggest difference to quality of life.

Original content ideas flow from journal publications, breaking news in the media, and the opinions of experts in areas where their work can make a real difference to the way people or organisations think or operate.

Creating content is also based on decisions around the timing of news, not only considering the external news agenda, but also when the institution's audience is most likely to be listening or searching for that type of content. Universities need to target many different audiences and at various times in their calendar year, so even a great piece of content can 'fail' if it is not released when its target audience is mostly likely to be listening.

AUDIENCE TARGETING

We judge how popular new content might be by trends in popular culture and the needs of the business.

For each story published online, tweet, blog post and video, we record the number of hits and retweets. We tend to use this as a measure of popularity, but it is also important to place these figures in the context of good/bad timing and connection to the wider news agenda. For example, we may not have considered producing a podcast to promote research two years ago, but with the increased demand for podcast production from research funders and its popularity overseas, we now see the value in this tool for communicating news to academic audiences and the wider public.

However, there are occasions where we have to produce new content ideas based on predictions of the funding environment. For example, if we know that there will be increased competition for funding in the area of antibiotic resistance research, then we will want to think creatively about content in this area, to demonstrate that our organisation is a major player in the field.

MITIGATING RISK

One of the ways we mitigate risk is by looking at media trends. For example, when science and health correspondents on the national newspapers started their own personal blogs, we knew that this could be a good outlet for research news, but also a place where journalists might source news. Another example is when research journals began to request video content for their major papers. This was a good indication that more people wanted to access research through film content.

It is important to be aware of the strengths of your closest competitors. If a particular organisation has dominated a research area for many years, but the funding environment dictates that we also have to communicate what we are doing in this area, then we will want to think creatively about how and when we release content about this topic, compared to the material that is already out there. This is when pitching exclusive stories to a journalist can be useful or thinking about less traditional media, such as podcasts, that might have a better chance of reaching a new audience.

FILTERING IDEAS

New content ideas are evaluated on how likely they are to generate media coverage; if they are an appropriate outlet for research; if they will reach our target audience; and if it will generate hits on our website.

Increasingly, we evaluate new ideas on where they fit within particular 'themes' that government bodies and funders are interested in. Instead of measuring the success of one news story on robotics, for example, we would look at how the piece of content has enhanced our overall visibility in the 'theme' of autonomous systems. News outlets are also looking at their stories more thematically, such as the BBC's week-long focus on mental health.

The measure of success here is whether our content would work for this theme across TV, online, radio and social media.

REACHING NEW AUDIENCES

In order to reach new audiences, research into the market is required in areas such as local economy, industry, internet engagement, education and media. If we wanted to target audiences in India, for example, we know that news focused on management, engineering, finance, and architecture is more likely to interest their press compared to stories in the arts disciplines, due to the number of students aiming to enter these professions.

Reaching audiences in different countries is always a challenge and this is where research on culture and media is really important. Not only do you need to gather intelligence on the awareness of your brand and where information about your organisation is sourced, but in the case of audiences in other countries, you need to know how your city and your country is represented too. This will help in pitching the right type of content at the right time.

MEASURING SUCCESS OF NEW INITIATIVES

Success of a new initiative can be measured by how many hits a story has online, compared to other news stories released that day; the number of retweets, likes on Instagram and Facebook, etc. We would also look at how extensive the media coverage was and the quality of the coverage in our target markets. In some cases we can be assured of success if a story prompts calls from industry looking for more information or potential collaboration opportunities.

It is important to measure success within context, however, and the time at which a piece of content is released factors into this. A particular Liverpool graduation story, for example, generated the most likes on Facebook compared to any piece of content released in that academic year. In order to truly understand its success you have to factor in the audience it was targeting and the fact that at this particular time a large volume of students and families would have been using social media to tell their own similar stories. Its success, therefore, was not necessarily more than any other story that year, but certainly the most successful at reaching its audience.

CHOOSING THE RIGHT CONTENT FORMAT

In the digital age, we speak of news stories as packages; it is not just about producing press releases anymore, but creating engaging copy for multiple platforms alongside photography, film and social media messages.

If a story works across all digital platforms and in more traditional media, such as newspapers and TV, then we will put considerable effort into making this content as accessible as possible. It goes without saying that stories with great visuals (photography and film), human interest, and an element of 'surprise' are more likely to work across multiple channels. The popularity of blogs has also made it easier to pitch stories around the profile of an individual. If we have a great research finding that we want to share, but we can also sell the researcher as a guest blogger on this research theme, then we ultimately maximise our visibility.

CHOOSING THE RIGHT PUBLISHING CHANNEL

The target audience influences where a piece of content is published. If we are promoting a complex science story we are less likely to target a regional tabloid newspaper, as it wouldn't be suitable for their audience or perhaps not suitable in print media. It might, however, get take-up by specialist correspondents on broadcast media or in the trade press, where it would reach a more academic audience.

A University has a diverse audience, from potential students, to researchers and industry partners, so a piece content on a new technology in the field of engineering, for example, is not going to be of interest to all of these audiences or at the same time, but we can maximise our research profile by choosing the right channel to disseminate our news and at the best time for our audience.

During the 'Welcome Week' season for students, for example, we know that research content on the organisation's news site is unlikely to be as successful compared to a strong student experience story. We wouldn't choose to launch a social media campaign about cancer research during A-level results week because the message would get lost amongst the volume of content concentrated around the student experience. We might, however, release a feature about an expert in cancer research who is teaching the next generation of medics, which could hit the research audience but also those students interested in studying medicine. It is ultimately about tailoring your best content to the right audience at the right time, through the channel they are most likely to engage with.

DESIGN: CLARE CURRAN

Clare Curran is an award-winning web designer, with 16 years' experience working with some of the biggest brands in the world, such as Coca-Cola, Toyota, Lexus, Saatchi & Saatchi, Virgin and Unilever. Her main fortes are concept visualisation, user experience design and motion graphics. Along with a range of exhibition work, Clare has had work published in various design publications, including *Creative Review* and *Mac Design Online*.

THINK-LOOK

When you think about the biggest brands in your world, whether it's Apple, Wal-Mart or Aston Martin, you'll automatically associate them with a set of visual identifiers. What do they look like? For Apple it might be clear, smooth imagery; for Wal-Mart, it might be no frills pale blues and yellow stars; for Aston Martin it might be the sleek, contemporary-classic style that springs to mind. Many of these visual identifiers don't come directly from our experience with these companies, but instead from how the product is positioned via other interactions we have with the brand, such as the content (and traditional marketing) they publish on TV, online and within stores. To a great extent, these brands have the power to control this mental imagery. The images you have in your head when you think about these brands have been placed there deliberately.

It's up to the brand to create a coherent image that its target customers will easily identify with. What visual identifiers do you want to stimulate when customers hear your name?

DYNAMIC GUIDELINES

The brands that stand the test of time are the ones that flex with their market. Regardless of whether it's a B2B or B2C scenario, the needs and desires of your customers are continually evolving. So, it makes sense for the representation of your brand to grow and develop over time with the market. One of the best ways to allow for fluidity, yet remain consistent in the overall message, is to employ dynamic brand guidelines. In other words, guidelines that take into account things like changing business objectives, advances in technology, emerging communication channels and lifestyle trends.

Whenever I'm involved with developing brand guidelines, I try to build in room for progress. It's almost like second guessing how the brand might evolve with the market. For example, think about how the brand guidelines you are developing would stand up if the business was to diversify or specialise its offering. How tied to the here and now is our branding?

It's not a secret that listening to customers is one of the simplest and most effective ways to stay in business! This also goes for brand guidelines. What do your customers think about how your brand is presented? Get their feedback directly by asking, but also indirectly by looking at sentiments in online conversations about your brand. The key here is to listen and judge which feedback can be dealt with over the course of the brand's development.

LOGO POWER

Countless studies have shown that people recognise and relate to images faster than text. Since your content marketing efforts aren't aiming to overtly sell, appropriately branding your owned media content, either subtly or explicitly with your logo can quickly and unmistakably link the content to your brand, without you ever mentioning your business.

But, let's take a step back for a moment. Ask yourself what your logo means to your brand and how does it relate to its place in the market. How does it represent what you stand for? Does it tell a story or make a statement about who you are? It's much more than just a graphic or font, it sets the whole tone of your messages. Your logo must be appropriate to your business and the market it's operating within. If it isn't, it's unlikely to have the impact you're hoping for when it appears alongside your content.

COLOUR YOUR WORLD

Never underestimate how important colours are to the messages you want to convey. Not only can colour set mood and perception, it can also help to pull together themes and packages of content.

Think about the main themes within your content strategy. What is the tone of the message? How does it fit together? I find it useful to create a colour palette that supports broader themes, with subtle variations. For example, if 'the environment' is one of your focuses, you might want to tie this in with earth shades like greens, yellows and browns.

Remember to specify a set of colours and tones, including hex values, CMYK and pantones. I often use a simple Adobe Photoshop template with opaque overlays to generate colour ranges that stem from one parent shade.

Figure 15: Example colour picker

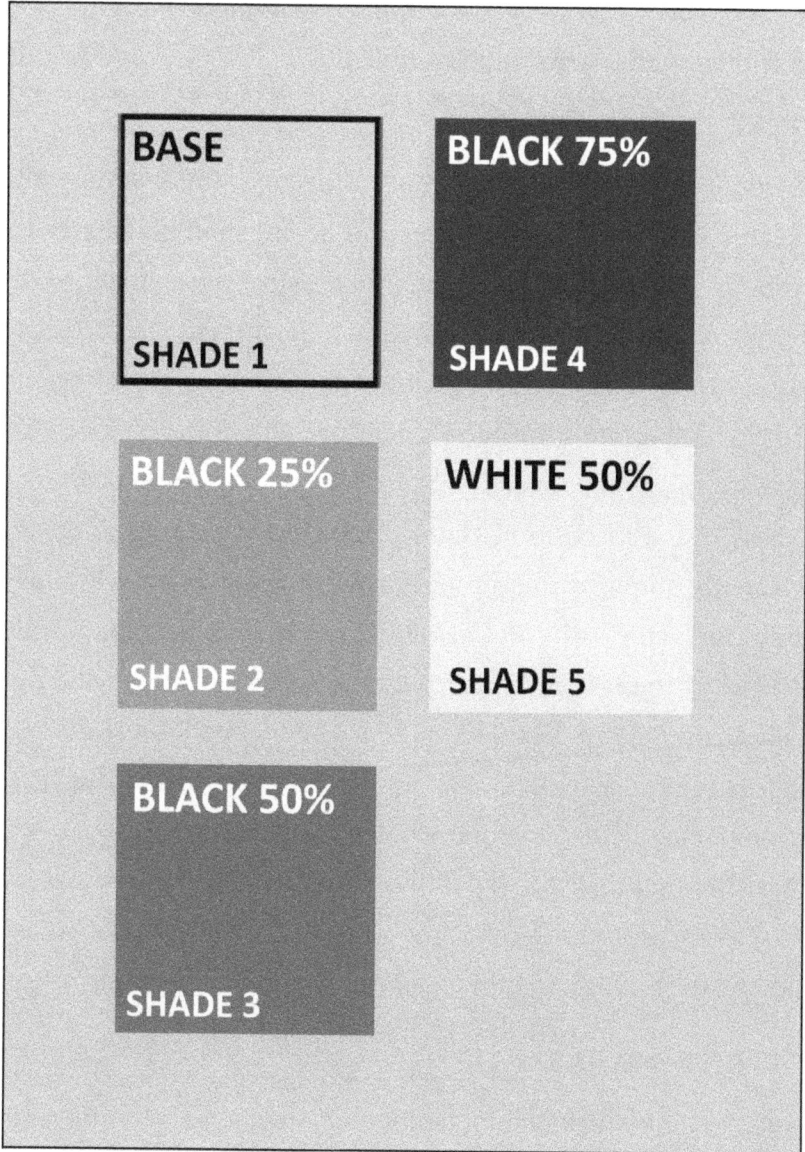

There's a downloadable version of this colour picker on the *Content Marketing Revolution* website (www.contentmarketingrevolution.com).

TYPICAL TYPOGRAPHY

If the words and tone are your brand's 'language', think of the font as its 'accent'. The typography you use across multiple channels and content types should be as consistent as possible. If you were wondering, the term 'typography' refers to the art and technique of arranging type to make written language readable and appealing.

It is important not to underestimate how important typography is to the overall coherency of your brand image, regardless of the medium of channel. Graphic design guru, Brian Hoff recently summed this up perfectly in an interview with Jad Limcaco for *Smashing Magazine*: "In school typography was always one of the last elements of design that students, including myself, learned and understood, but once understood can really set you apart from others. Great design can be lost with bad typography."

Bear in mind that the way different fonts render online and in print will vary according to format and size, so always test which should be used online and offline, along with sizes for specific uses.

THE RIGHT IMAGES

It's true that a picture paints a thousand words, so what do you want those words to say? Again, identify key themes and specify the types of photography (or even specific photographs) that send out the right messages. How do you want people and places to be represented? Think about the mood of the photography in relation to the messages you want to convey.

Look at some of the biggest brands in the world, such as Starbucks, Samsung and Gillette and you'll notice how distinctive the photography is to their brand's look and feel across publications, videos, marketing collateral and even social media.

AVOIDING 'PRETTY AWFUL'

Remember the objective of each piece of content and don't get lost in the idea of creating a pretty piece of work. Of course we want our work to look visually appealing, but even the best designed and presented content is still going to be pretty awful if there is no quality or substance in the message. Always be led by the objective of the content and invest valuable design time in all of the right places. Think impact, think reputation but, most importantly, think purpose.

GLOSSARY

AFFINITY DIAGRAMS

An 'affinity diagram' (also known as 'affinity' chart or the 'KJ Method') is a tool used to organise ideas and data by sorting them into groups.

ATTITUDINAL VARIABLES

'Attitudinal variables' are representations of the feelings a specific group of people have on a particular topic. These attitudes (such as likes and dislikes) are usually derived from surveys and interviews with a sample set of people, which can then be mapped across a spectrum.

BIG AIM

The overarching purpose of the strategy as a whole is known as the 'big aim'. This is the primary focus of what the mission sets out to accomplish. The big aim should be supported by a series of supporting goals, which are then subsequently split into objectives and tactics.

BUSINESS CASE

The 'business case' is a formal argument (usually both written and presented in-person) for pursuing a specific course of action, using examples and supporting information. The business case is targeted towards the key decision maker(s) in an organisation.

BUYER PERSONAS

'Buyer personas' (also known as 'customer personas') are fictional characters that are created to represent real customer or audience groups. Personas aim to represent customer types, grouped according to their needs and motivations. They are used for a variety of purposes in marketing, such as customer targeting and user experience planning for digital projects.

BUYER'S JOURNEY

The 'buyer's journey' is made up of the stages that every customer goes through before buying a product, from becoming aware of their need to making a purchase. Although not all customers will spend the same amount of time at each stage, the process will largely be the same.

CONTENT AMPLIFICATION

Promoting, highlighting and marketing content in order to reach the largest possible audience across one or more publishing channels is known as 'Content amplification'.

CONTENT AUDIT

A 'content audit' is the evaluation of all content within a specific portfolio, usually including individual quality assessment and specific recommendations. A content audit is usually conducted in conjunction with a 'content inventory' (see below).

CONTENT CALENDAR

A 'content calendar' is a plan that specifies production and publication dates of content over a period of time. Content calendars vary in complexity and formats (paper-based or web/software-based), usually according to the volume and scale of the schedule.

CONTENT COMMUNITY

The 'content community' is a collection of individuals, groups or brands that have an interest in a specific topic. A content community typically includes customers, product or brand champions and competitors.

CONTENT CURATION

Gathering, filtering and selectively republishing content that has been produced by a third-party is known as 'content curation'. The content must not be republished in its entirety and the terms of publishing should be beneficial to both the original publisher and the curator.

CONTENT FORMAT

The 'content format' is the technical make-up of the content, e.g. PDF, print, webpage, MP3. Not to be confused with 'content type' (see below).

CONTENT INVENTORY

A 'content inventory' is a complete catalogue of the entire contents of a website, including a record of whether the content is currently published and its location. A content inventory is usually conducted in conjunction with a 'content audit' (see above).

CONTENT MARKETING

The term 'content marketing' refers to marketing activities that involve the creation and distribution of useful or stimulating content in order to acquire and retain customers, without overtly selling a product or brand.

CONTENT NICHE

A 'content niche' is the highly-specific topic specialism that a publisher focuses attention on. Publishers tend to focus on niche topics in order to influence customer attitudes and needs, while gaining authority in an area that aligns with their specific knowledge or expertise.

CONTENT TYPE

The 'content type' is the kind of content that is being published, e.g. blog post, web page, video, whitepaper or leaflet. The content type is not to be confused with the 'content format' (see above).

CONVERGED MEDIA

'Converged media' is content that is amplified (or distributed) through a combination of at least two amplification methods, e.g. paid media, owned media and/or earned media.

EARNED MEDIA

The term 'earned media' (also known as 'free media') refers to content that is amplified (or distributed) through publicity, editorial influence and other promotional tactics that are not paid for. Examples include: news articles, features and social shares, mentions and reposts.

INFLUENCERS

'Influencers' are individuals, groups and brands that have dominant voices in their field. Their ideas and views have the power to shape other people's opinions and drive actions.

OWNED MEDIA

'Owned media' is content that is amplified (or distributed) across channels that are within your control, such as websites, blogs, or email. Typically, owned media is free to publish. Examples include: content published to proprietary websites, apps, blogs and social channels.

PAID MEDIA

Content that is amplified (or distributed) with paid-for advertising or promotion is known as 'paid media'. Examples include: pay-per-click, display advertising, sponsored posts, paid influencers, social media advertisements and retargeting.

PUBLISHING CHANNELS

The places content is published, such as websites, blog sites, email and social platforms such as Facebook, Twitter, and YouTube, are known as 'publishing channels'.

REAL-TIME PUBLISHING

The term 'real-time publishing' refers to agile content production and publishing that typically aim to influence customer conversations as they happen. Real-time publishing is influenced by current trends and developing topics within specific topic areas.

SEARCH ENGINE OPTIMISATION

The term 'search engine optimisation' refers to the process of maximising the number of visitors to a particular website or piece of content. This typically includes effectively using relevant keywords in a structure and format that search engines, such as Google, will recognise as relevant targeted search queries.

SOCIAL MEDIA

Websites and applications that enable users to create and share content or to participate in social networking are known as 'social media'.

STYLE GUIDE

A 'style guide' (also sometimes known as 'brand standards') is a set of guidelines to help publishers create content that is consistent in look, quality, tone and appearance. These guidelines typically include basic information about editorial uniformity, brand personality and visual identity.

REFERENCE LINKS

1. ABC, http://abc.go.com

2. AddThis, http://www.addthis.com

3. Altimeter, http://www.altimetergroup.com

4. Any Meeting, http://www.anymeeting.com

5. Ask MetaFilter, http://ask.metafilter.com

6. BBC, http://www.bbc.co.uk

7. Blaze, http://www.blazecontent.com

8. Book Baby, http://www.bookbaby.com

9. BrandWatch, http://www.brandwatch.com

10. Burns & McDonnell, http://www.burnsmcd.com

11. Buyer Persona Manifesto, http://www.buyerpersona.com

12. Cam Studio, http://www.camstudio.org

13. CBS, http://www.cbs.com

14. Cision, http://www.cision.com

15. Click Webinar, http://www.clickwebinar.com

16. Clickz, http://www.clickz.com

17. CNN, http://www.cnn.com

18. Coca-Cola, http://www.coca-cola.com

19. Content Marketing Institute,

     http://www.contentmarketinginstitute.com

20. Content Marketing Revolution,

     http://www.contentmarketingrevolution.com

21. Contently, http://www.contently.com

22. Convince and Convert,

     http://www.convinceandconvert.com

23. Create Space, http://www.createspace.com

24. Curata, http://www.curata.com

25. Delicious, http://www.delicious.com

26. DemandGen, http://www.demandgen.com

27. DemandMetric, http://www.demandmetric.com

28. Digg, http://www.digg.com

29. Eloqua, http://www.eloqua.com

30.   Facebook, http://www.facebook.com

31.   Feedley, http://www.feedly.com

32.   Four Seasons Hotels and Resorts,

      http://www.fourseasons.com

33.   Gather Content, http://www.gathercontent.com

34.   Gillette, http://www.gillette.com

35.   Go Animate, http://www.goanimate.com

36.   Google Alerts, http://www.google.co.uk/alerts

37.   Google Analytics, http://www.google.co.uk/analytics

38.   Google Docs, http://www.google.co.uk/docs/about/

39.   Google Keyword Planner,

      http://adwords.google.com/keywordplanner

40.   Google Plus, http://plus.google.com

41.   Google Trends, http://www.google.co.uk/trends

42.   Hasbro, http://www.hasbro.com

43.   HBO, http://www.hbo.com

44.   Hootsuite, http://www.hootsuite.com

45. Hubspot, http://www.hubsot.com

46. Imgflip, http:// www.imgflip.com

47. IMN, http://www.imninc.com

48. Infogram, http://www.infogr.am

49. Instagram, http//www.instagram.com

50. ITV, http://www.itv.com

51. Jell-O, http://www.jello.com

52. John Deere, http://www.deere.com

53. Klout, http://www.klout.com

54. LEGO, http://www.lego.com

55. Lexus, http://www.lexus.com

56. LinkedIn, http://www.linkedin.com

57. LinkedIn Technology Marketing Community,
     http://www.linkedin.com/groups/B2B-Technology-
     Marketing-Community-43707/about

58. LookBookHQ, http://www.lookbookhq.com

59. MailChimp, http://www.mailchimp.com

60. Marketing Profs, http://www.marketingprofs.com

61. Marketo, http://www.marketo.com

62. Marvel, http://www.marvel.com

63. Meerkat, http://www.meerkatapp.co

64. Meme Generator, http://www.memegenerator.net

65. Mention, http://www.en.mention.com

66. Michelin, http://www.michelin.com

67. MTV, http://www.mtv.com

68. NBC, http://www.nbc.com

69. Netvibes, http://www.netvibes.com

70. Open University, http://www.open.ac.uk

71. Outbrain, http://www.outbrain.com

72. Paper.li, http://www.paper.li

73. Philips, http://www.philips.com

74. Picture Vision Pictures,

    http://www.picturevisionpictures.com

75. Piktochart, http://www.piktochart.com

76. Pinterest, http:http://www.pinterest.com

77. Pixton, http://www.pixton.com

78. Pure 360, http://www.pure360.com

79. QuickSprout, http://www.quicksprout.com

80. Quora, http://www.quora.com

81. Radian6, http://www.radian6.com

82. Red Bull, http://www.redbull.com

83. Russell Group, http://www.russellgroup.ac.uk

84. Saatchi and Saatchi, http://www.saatchi.com

85. Salesforce, http://www.salesforce.com

86. Samsung, http:www.samsung.com

87. ScoopIt, http://www.scoop.it

88. Scouse Bird Problems,

    http://www.scousebirdproblems.com

89. Screaming Frog, http://www.screamingfrog.co.uk

90. Screencast-O-Matic, http://www.screencast-o-matic.com

91. SEMrush, http://www.semrush.com

92. Shared Count, http://www.sharedcount.com

93. Showtime, http://www.sho.com

94. SlideShare, http://www.slideshare.net

95. Social Media Examiner,

    http://www.socialmediaexaminer.com

96. Social Mention, http://www.socialmention.com

97. Socialcrawlytics, http://www.socialcrawlytics.com

98. Starbucks, http://www.starbucks.com

99. Static Brain, http://www.statisticbrain.com

100. Swayy, http://www.swayy.co

101. Talkwalker Alerts, http://www.talkwalker.com/alerts

102. The Guardian, http://www.theguardian.com

103. The Times, http://www.thetimes.com

104. The Tweeted Times, http://www.tweetedtimes.com

105. Tourism Australia, http://www.australia.com

106. Toyota, http://www.toyota-global.com

107. Traackr, http://www.traackr.com

108. TrapIt, http://www.trap.it

109. Twitter, http://www.twitter.com

110. Unilever, http://www.unilever.com

111. University of Liverpool, http://www.liverpool.ac.uk

112. Unsplash, http://www.unsplash.com

113. Vimeo, http://www.vimeo.com

114. Virgin, http://www.virgin.com

115. Web Trends, http://www.webtrends.com

116. Wordtracker, http://www.wordtracker.com

117. Yale University, http://www.yale.edu

118. YouTube Live Events,

    http://www.youtube.com/my_live_events

119. YouTube, http://www.youtube.com

120. Zemanta, http://www.zemanta.com

121. Zoho, http://www.zoho.com

ACKNOWLEDGEMENTS

There are so many people I would like to thank for their inspiration, support and patience while I've been writing this book.

Firstly, I'd like to thank Matt Warnock at Philips for taking time out of his busy schedule to write the foreword. What a privilege it is to have your words opening the book.

For generously imparting some of their extensive wisdom and experience, I would like to thank Debora Fougere, Samantha Martin, Mark Davies Markham, Alexander Birrell and Clare Curran. I'm honoured to have your contributions within these pages.

For their support at various stages of the project, I would also like to offer my thanks to Mike Claridge, Mark Langshaw, Adele Revella and Jo Banks.

The whole process of writing my first book would have been much more difficult without the support of my family:

For her strength of character, dedication and the work ethic she instilled upon me, I would like to thank my mother, Pauline. You have always been an inspiration to me.

Writing this book would not have been possible without the influence of my grandfather, Alf, and grandmother, Irene. Thank you for everything you taught me over the years, not least about commitment and dedication. I miss you both every day.

For her unwavering support and belief in me, I would like to thank my grandmother, Josephine. It was your stories over the years that first inspired me to write.

ACKNOWLEDGEMENTS

For encouraging my creativity and listening to my ideas, not least during the early stages of this book, I would like to thank my father, Anton.

Thank you to my brothers, Ricky and Kyle, for being constant sources of support and inspiration. Ricky, I thank you for your fine example, integrity and guidance. Kyle, your talent, ambition and strong will are like guiding lights.

Finally, no words on this page could ever express how grateful I am to Rachel for her patience, support and impeccable judgement.

CONNECT WITH DANE

Website : www.danebrookes.com

Twitter: @danebrookes

ABOUT THE AUTHOR

Dane Brookes is a content marketing and communications specialist, with a broad range of experience that has touched many different sectors and industries.

With a background in business journalism and content strategy, he has produced high-profile marketing and communications campaigns for some of the most influential global brands of the last decade.

At the forefront of the open-access boom, Dane led an editorial department at one of the world's largest publishing houses, before going on to manage digital marketing and communications for a number of high-profile organisations, including a national housing charity, a Russell Group university and a FTSE 100 utility company.

In 2012, he founded marketing and technology company, Group Dane (www.groupdane.com), which has a portfolio of clients in the UK, USA and Europe.

www.ingramcontent.com/pod-product-compliance
Lightning Source LLC
Chambersburg PA
CBHW020153200326
41521CB00006B/350